ID0820330

PRACTICAL GUIDE TO CLINICAL COMPUTING SYSTEMS: DESIGN, OPERATIONS, AND INFRASTRUCTURE

PRACTICAL GUIDE TO CLINICAL COMPUTING SYSTEMS: DESIGN, OPERATIONS, AND INFRASTRUCTURE

EDITED BY

THOMAS H. PAYNE
UW Medicine Information Technology Services
University of Washington
Seattle, WA

AMSTERDAM • BOSTON • HEIDELBERG • LONDON
NEW YORK • OXFORD • PARIS • SAN DIEGO
SAN FRANCISCO • SINGAPORE • SYDNEY • TOKYO

Academic Press is an imprint of Elsevier

Academic Press is an imprint of Elsevier
84 Theobald's Road, London WC1X 8RR, UK
Linacre House, Jordan Hill, Oxford OX2 8DP, UK
Radarweg 29, PO Box 211, 1000 AE Amsterdam, The Netherlands
30 Corporate Drive, Suite 400, Burlington, MA 01803, USA
525 B Street, Suite 1900, San Diego, CA 92101-4495, USA

First edition 2008

Notice
No responsibility is assumed by the publisher for any injury and/or damage to persons
or property as a matter of products liability, negligence or otherwise, or from any use
or operation of any methods, products, instructions or ideas contained in the material
herein. Because of rapid advances in the medical sciences, in particular, independent
verification of diagnoses and drug dosages should be made

British Library Cataloguing-in-Publication Data
A catalogue record for this book is available from the British Library

Library of Congress Cataloging-in-Publication Data
A catalog record for this book is available from the Library of Congress

ISBN: 978-0-12-374002-1

For information on all Academic Press publications
visit our website at books.elsevier.com

Printed and bound in USA
08 09 10 11 12   10 9 8 7 6 5 4 3 2 1

To Molly, Jenny, and Amy

CONTENTS

CONTRIBUTORS

Sally Beahan, RHIA (171)

Director, Patient Data Services
University of Washington Medical Center
Seattle, Washington

David Chou, MD, MS (37)

Chief Technical Officer, IT Services
UW Medicine
Director, Informatics and Associate Professor
Department of Laboratory Medicine
University of Washington
Seattle, Washington

John Doulis, MD (105)

Chief Operations Officer, Informatics Center
Assistant Vice Chancellor
Vanderbilt University
Nashville, Tennessee

Matt Eisenberg, MD (129)

Informatics Physician
Children's Hospital and Regional Medical Center
M3-2–Medical Informatics
Seattle, Washington

James Fine, MD (181)

Executive Director, Clinical Computing
UW Medicine
Chairman and Associate Professor
Department of Laboratory Medicine
University of Washington
Seattle, Washington

Grant Fletcher, MD, MPH (181)

Assistant Professor
Department of Medicine
Division of General Internal Medicine
Harborview Medical Center
University of Washington
Seattle, Washington

Wendy Giles, RN, BSN (81, 97)

EMR Director, IT Services
UW Medicine
Seattle, Washington

James Hoath (25)

Director, Clinical Architecture, IT Services
UW Medicine
Seattle, Washington

Patty Hoey, RPh (129)

Lead Clinical Application Coordinator
VA Puget Sound Health Care System
Seattle, Washington

David Masuda, MD, MS (195)

Lecturer
Department of Medical Education and Biomedical Informatics
School of Medicine
University of Washington
Seattle, Washington

Thomas Payne, MD, FACP, FACMI (1, 13, 25)

Medical Director, IT Services
UW Medicine
Clinical Associate Professor
Departments of Medicine, Health Services
and Medical Education & Biomedical Informatics
University of Washington
Seattle, Washington

Soumitra Sengupta, PhD (37)

Information Security Officer
NewYork-Presbyterian Hospital and Columbia University Medical Center
Assistant Clinical Professor
Department of Biomedical Informatics
Columbia University
New York, NY

Benjamin A. "Jamie" Trigg, PMP (105)

Manager, Clinical Application Support
IT Services
UW Medicine
Seattle, Washington

Jacquie Zehner, RHIT (159)

Director, Patient Data Services
Harborview Medical Center
Seattle, Washington

PREFACE

This book is intended for those in graduate or fellowship training in informatics who intend to have informatics careers and for those who find themselves adding informatics to their existing responsibilities. I've noticed that many informatics trainees know less than they should about the practical side of clinical computing, such as the realities of building HL7 interfaces, interface engines, and ongoing support; yet many will enter careers in which part of their time will be devoted to informatics operations in a medical center. We also hope to help those working in medical centers who find themselves appointed to a committee or leadership position for clinical computing. As organizations install clinical computing applications, they need knowledgeable clinicians to guide their organization through the process.

There are many good articles and books covering implementation of clinical computing systems. However, most of our time and energy will be spent keeping existing systems operating. This means infrastructure such as networks, servers, training and supporting users, installing updates, preparing for Joint Commission reviews, keeping the medical record intact, and myriad other tasks that will continue indefinitely, long after the adrenaline-filled days of implementation have passed.

The idea for this book arose in a seminar series at the University of Washington titled "Operating Clinical Computing Systems in a Medical Center" that has been offered each spring since 2005. Seminar presenters have operational responsibility for clinical computing systems at UW and elsewhere, and we combine seminars with tours of patient care areas and computing equipment rooms to give participants a sense of what this field is like for clinician-users and those who spend their days and nights keeping the systems operational. We invited experts from some other leading medical centers to contribute their experience to the book, with the understanding that no single hospital has the best solutions to all aspects of this field. While reading this book, we encourage readers to learn about this field by experiencing clinical computing in to the real world of ICUs, wards, and clinics, which is the best teacher of all. Please send us your feedback, questions, and suggestions.

Thomas H Payne
Seattle

1

INTRODUCTION AND OVERVIEW OF CLINICAL COMPUTING SYSTEMS WITHIN A MEDICAL CENTER

THOMAS PAYNE

IT Services, UW Medicine, Departments of Medicine, Health Services, and Medical Education & Biomedical Informatics, University of Washington, Seattle, WA

Clinical computing systems—defined computing systems used in direct patient care—are commonplace in health-care organizations and growing in importance. Clinical laboratories and hospital business offices were the first to adopt computing systems within hospitals, but today electronic medical record systems (EMRs) and computerized practitioner order entry (CPOE) have been installed in many medical centers and are integrally tied to clinical care. Most medical centers could not operate efficiently without automated patient registration, results review, pharmacy, and other clinical computing systems.

It's challenging to install clinical computing systems such as electronic medical record systems, but it is arguably even more difficult to keep them continuously available, 24 hours every day, even at 2 am on New Year's Day. Operating these systems over the long term requires planning for expansion, replacing hardware, hiring and training staff, promptly helping clinicians with application questions, avoiding and correcting network outages, upgrading hardware and software, creating new interfaces between systems, and myriad other tasks that are often unnoticed by clinicians who use them. Yet these tasks must be accomplished to continue to accrue advantages from sophisticated clinical computing systems.

The informatics literature focuses great deal of attention to implementing clinical computing systems, and managing the change this entails. This is not surprising, since the transition from paper to electronic systems is usually more difficult than expected. Much less attention has been devoted to the critical tasks involved in keeping systems continuously running and available to their users. This requires understanding of long-term issues—the marathon of continuous, reliable operation rather than the sprint of implementation.

Successfully operating clinical computing systems is easier if you learn the fundamentals of how they work, even if you recruit and hire people who know more about the fundamentals than you do. All those involved in the long-term operation of clinical computing systems may benefit from this fundamental background. That is the purpose of this book: To help readers learn about the design, operations, governance, regulation, staffing, and other practical aspects essential to successfully operating clinical computing systems within a health-care organization.

THE HEALTH-CARE SETTING

Healthcare is delivered in many settings, but in this book we will concentrate on medical centers and large clinics. Both of these settings have higher volumes and pace than was true 20 years ago. For example, Harborview Medical Center and the University of Washington Medical Center in Seattle, Washington where many of this book's authors are based, are filled beyond their designed capacity many days each year. Harborview's average occupancy in 2006 was 97%. Emergency room volumes are rising, with 50–70 of the 300 patients seen at Harborview Medical Center daily ill enough to warrant immediate admission. The number of intensive care unit beds is rising at both Harborview and UW Medical Center, because of increasing need to care for critically ill patients. The pressure of hospitals filled to capacity leads to more patients being treated in clinics or the emergency room, and as a consequence clinics treat more complicated medical problems than in the past. The pressure of high patient volumes along with pressures to constrain health-care costs and to improve quality and efficiency have led many organizations to turn to approaches used successfully in other sectors of society, including process improvement techniques and adoption of information technology.

RISING DEPENDENCE ON CLINICAL COMPUTING SYSTEMS

The volume of information clinicians use in day-to-day care has risen over the last 50 years. Imaging studies such as chest films are increasingly acquired, stored and displayed in digital form. Computerized tomography and magnetic resonance imaging studies have always been acquired digitally. As the number and resolution of these patient images has risen, picture archiving and communication systems (PACS) are commonly used instead of folders containing acetate xray films. Paper records are commonly scanned and displayed on workstations. Physicians, nurses, and others are increasingly entering notes electronically and reading medical records using EMRs. Laboratories and pharmacies have long used computing systems to manage their departments. Critical care units capture enormous volumes of patient information such as vascular pressures, mechanical ventilator data, heart monitoring data, and other information from bedside devices. Often these data are gathered, summarized, and displayed for clinicians using computing systems. Because of pressures from patient volumes, acuity, and reimbursement rules, there are strong incentives to manage and act on clinical information rapidly and efficiently; clinical computing systems help make this possible. As a consequence, many hospital leaders feel that fundamental hospital operations depend on reliable availability of clinical computing systems. It simply would not be possible to deliver care to as many patients or to efficiently manage a medical center if paper systems alone were used on wards, intensive care units, and support departments.

THE IMPORTANCE OF COMPUTING OPERATIONS AND SUPPORT

Because of this dependence, medical informatics has an increasingly important practical side. This has been true for decades, but clinical computing operations have become even more critical as paper-based patient care processes are automated. CPOE, electronic documentation, bar coded administration of medication, PACS systems, results review, remote access, ICU systems, and others have increased clinicians' dependence on reliable, fast access to clinical computing systems. Phrases such as "five 9s," long familiar to the telecommunications industry, are now heard in hospitals to signify standards for availability far above 99.9% of the time, which would leave clinicians without their systems 0.1% of the time, or 43 minutes each month.

It is important to develop or select, configure, and install clinical computing systems successfully, but to the degree that clinicians grow to depend on them, continuous availability becomes more important. The need for reliable clinical computing systems continues long after the satisfaction with initial installation has come and gone. The bar is continuously being raised, and once raised, it is not lowered without disruption and upsetting clinicians. Hospitals and clinics have rising volumes and pressure for increased productivity, which computing systems can help.

Backup systems must be present to protect against unplanned system downtime. But backup systems are no substitute for system reliability, because moving to and from backup systems carries risk. To the degree that systems are more reliable, paper backup systems may become unfamiliar to medical center staff. The transition to and from paper backup systems can create harm. For example, when a downtime affects entry of orders, orders that were in the process of being entered when downtime occurred are not received by the filling department. The clinician may delay entering more orders because of uncertainty over whether the electronic CPOE system will soon be brought back online. If the assessment is that the downtime will last longer than the organizational threshold to move to paper ordering, then the clinician may decide to reenter orders on paper and continue doing so until the announcement that the CPOE system is again available for order entry. Orders that had been entered on paper may then be "back entered" so that the electronic order list is again complete. During the transition from electronic to paper, and then from paper to electronic orders, order transmission is delayed, and there is a risk that orders will either be missed or entered twice, either of which could be hazardous to patients. Though procedures are usually in place to reduce risk of these hazards, if 10 000 orders are entered each day in the organization (seven orders each minute) and there are 3 hour-long unscheduled downtimes a year, the likelihood of error-free communication of all 1260 orders entered during these downtimes is low.

Causes for system outages are highly variable. For the last 6 years, I have logged e-mails I receive describing clinical computing system problems that have affected University of Washington clinical areas, and though my log is incomplete, there are over 1110 entries. Causes include construction mishaps severing cables between our hospitals, technical staff entering commands into the wrong terminal session on a workstation, air conditioning system failures, users mistakenly plugging two ends of a network cable into adjacent wall ports, denial of service attacks launched from virus-infected servers on our hospital wards, planned downtime for switch to daylight savings time, and many others. The health-care system has much to learn from the aviation industry's safety advances. Jumbo jet flights are safe because of a combination of standards, simplified engine design (turbine rather than piston engines), rigorously followed checklists and policies, redundancy, careful system monitoring, and many other advances learned from meticulous investigation when things go wrong. Medical center clinical computing systems can be made to be safer and more reliable by using the same approaches, yet we are only beginning to do so.

With each new clinical computing application or upgrade, complexity rises, and the infrastructure on which these systems rests carries a higher burden. When one studies these systems and learns from those who keep them running how complex they are, it leaves one with a sense of amazement that they run as well as they do. This is coupled with an impression that only through discipline and systematic approaches can we hope to have the reliability we expect. Yet there are no randomized controlled trials to guide us to the best way to select a clinical computing system, how to implement it, how to organize the information technology department, or to answer many other important questions that may help achieve reliable operations.

IMPORTANCE OF MONITORING PERFORMANCE

Even when clinical computing systems are running, they need to be continuously monitored to assure that application speed experienced by users is as it should be. Slow performance impairs worker productivity and may be a harbinger of system problems to come that require technical intervention to avoid. Experienced organizations know that application speed is one of the most important criteria for user satisfaction, and monitor their systems to assure they remain fast.

There is a continuum, rather than a sharp divide, between computing systems being available and "down." As performance declines, users must wait longer for information on screens to appear. As this delay increases from seconds to minutes, the applications are no longer practical to use even though they are technically "up."

REAL-WORLD PROBLEMS AND THEIR IMPLICATIONS

For a clinician to view a simple piece of information on her patient such as the most recent hematocrit, many steps must work without fail. The patient must be accurately identified and the blood sample must be linked to her. The laboratory processing the specimen must have a functioning computing system, and the network connection between the laboratory computer and clinical data repository where the patient's data are stored must be intact. The computing system that directs the result to be sent to the repository—an interface engine in many organizations—must also be functional. The master patient index that clearly identifies the patient as the same person in the laboratory and clinical data repository must have assigned the same identifier to both systems. Once the hematocrit result is stored in the clinical data repository, the clinician must have access to it from a functioning workstation which has accepted her password when she logged in. The clinical data repository must be running, and be functioning with sufficiently brisk response time that it is deemed usable at that moment. And the network segments that connect the clinician's workstation to the repository must be functioning. In some organizations, what the clinician sees on her workstation is not an application running on the workstation in front of her, but rather a screen painted by another computer that makes it appear as though she is running the clinical computing system on her workstation. (This arrangement saves the information technology team the effort of installing and updating the clinical computing application on thousands of workstations.) If this is the case, then the system responsible for painting the screen on her workstation must also be operational.

With this many moving parts required to view a single result, it is not surprising that things go wrong, nor that the consequences of clinical computing system outages are significant for medical centers [1]. Monitoring all of these systems to detect problems is extremely challenging: Network availability throughout the campus, status of the laboratory system, interface engine, core clinical data repository, workstation availability, and response time for all of these systems must all be within boundaries acceptable to busy clinicians 24 hours a day, every day of the year. Monitoring and identifying problems that might interfere with the ability of the clinician to see the hematocrit result, ideally before the clinician is aware a problem exists, is very difficult. Over time, some organizations have developed the strategy of placing "robot users" in patient care areas to repetitively look up results or place orders on fictitious patients just as a clinician would, and set off alarms for support personnel if the hematocrit doesn't appear within acceptable boundaries of performance. When an alarm occurs, each of the possible causes—from power outage to network hardware on that ward to a system wide outage of core systems— must be rapidly investigated and rectified. Data from these robots can also track performance changes close to those seen by users to guide system tuning or to plan hardware enhancements. Some organizations rely on users themselves to report performance decline or loss of service, but this strategy may not work if problems are intermittent, gradual, occur in infrequently used areas, or if busy clinicians delay reporting outages they assume are already known to system administrators.

INTRODUCING CLINICAL COMPUTING SYSTEMS CAN INTRODUCE ERRORS

Using clinical computing systems solves many problems and can make care safer [2–4] and more efficient [5], but using these systems also carries risk. Exactly how clinicians will use them is hard to predict. Any powerful tool that can help solve problems can also introduce them. No matter how carefully designed and implemented, a system that can communicate orders for powerful medications has potential to cause harm by delay or by permitting the user to make new types of errors that are rapidly communicated to and carried out by pharmacists, radiologists, or others.

Examples in the literature show that the introduction of CPOE (along with other interventions) was associated with a rise in mortality rates for at least one group of patients in one medical center [6]. Another paper reported anecdotes of physicians using the CPOE system in ways it wasn't designed to be used, potentially introducing errors [7]. Changing the way clinicians review results, or dividing the results between multiple systems, can lead a clinician to miss a result that could potentially affect patient-care decisions. We know that all medications—even those with enormous potential benefit—can have adverse effects. It is not surprising that clinical computing systems do too. We need to keep this in mind and avoid complacency. Causing harm to patients during transition from paper to clinical computing system is possible, even likely. However, many organizations have chosen to adopt clinical computing systems and CPOE because of compelling evidence that our patients may be safer after the transition is accomplished.

WE NEED GREATER EMPHASIS ON SAFE OPERATIONS OF CLINICAL COMPUTING SYSTEMS

When problems with clinical computing systems occur, we need to report them, find out what happened, and take steps to assure that the same problem is unlikely to recur. At the University of Washington, we have begun reporting IT problems and near misses through the University Healthcare Consortium Patient Safety Net, in the same way we report medication errors and other problems. IT problems can and do affect patients, just as they can and do help patients. And just as we bring multidisciplinary teams together to find the root cause of problems and to correct the systems causing them, we all need to have better understanding of the root cause of IT problems and take informed steps to make problems less likely. This book can provide some of that understanding of how clinical computing systems work.

Clinical computing systems can offer improvements in patient safety, quality, and organizational efficiency. Medical centers are heavily reliant on them to make it possible to care for hospitals filled to capacity. The clinical computing systems and infrastructure are enormously complex and becoming more so, and they must operate reliably nearly continuously. Clinicians are busy delivering care with little time for training and low tolerance for malfunctioning systems. Security and accrediting groups carefully observe our custody of vital, personal health information. For all these reasons and others, it is therefore important that we have trained and experienced people who understand healthcare, information technology, health information regulations, and how to keep clinical computing systems reliably operating. It is for these reasons that we have written this book.

REFERENCES

[1] Kilbridge P. Computer crash–lessons from a system failure. N Engl J Med. 2003; 348(10): 881–2.

[2] Bates DW, Leape LL, Cullen DJ, et al. Effect of computerized physician order entry and a team intervention on prevention of serious medication errors. JAMA. 1998; 280: 1311–16.

[3] McDonald CJ. Protocol-based computer reminders, the quality of care and the non-perfectability of man. N Engl J Med. 1976; 295: 1351–5.

[4] Johnston ME, Langton KB, Haynes RB, et al. Effects of computer-based clinical decision support systems on clinician performance and patient outcome. A critical appraisal of research. Ann Intern Med. 1994; 120: 135–42.

[5] Tierney WM, McDonald CJ, Martin DK, et al. Computerized display of past test results. Effect on outpatient testing. Ann Intern Med. 1987; 107: 569–74.

[6] Han YY, Carcillo JA, Venkataraman ST, et al. Unexpected increased mortality after implementation of a commercially sold computerized physician order entry system [published correction appears in Pediatrics. 2006; 117: 594]. Pediatrics. 2005; 116: 1506–12.

[7] Koppel R, Metlay JP, Cohen A, et al. Role of computerized physician order entry systems in facilitating medication errors. JAMA. 2005; 293: 1197–203.

PART

I

DESIGN OF CLINICAL COMPUTING SYSTEMS

2

ARCHITECTURE OF CLINICAL COMPUTING SYSTEMS

THOMAS PAYNE

*IT Services, UW Medicine, Departments of Medicine, Health Services,
and Medical Education & Biomedical Informatics, University of Washington,
Seattle, WA*

WHAT IS ARCHITECTURE, AND WHY IS IT IMPORTANT?

To build a medical center requires expertise in engineering, human factors, design, medicine, and also architecture. It is the architect who melds design and function with engineering and practicality. We look to the architect to keep parts functioning together, and to plan for changes and additions that fit with the original design. Similarly, clinical computing systems have an architecture and often an architect behind them. Particularly in an era when most organizations license software from multiple computing system vendors, it is important to maintain an overall architecture to meet the organization's current and future needs.

The purpose of this chapter is to give an overview of the fundamentals of clinical computing system architectures commonly used at the time of publication of this book. This hasn't changed substantially since the late 1980s when data exchange between systems became more common and standards to permit this exchange were increasingly used. This is by no means to imply that better ways to arrange computing aren't possible—it is the authors' hope that better clinical computing architectures will be developed and adopted. But today, in most medical centers, what we describe here is often the way the architecture is designed and used.

ARCHITECTURAL MODELS

The simplest clinical computing system architecture is a single system, with a single database in which all data are shared between applications such as patient registration, laboratory, radiology, and others. Such a system may be developed within the organization or licensed from a single vendor. Early in the history of clinical computing this model was common. Applications may have been based on a single vendor's hardware and database management systems, with new applications added as new screens or small applications within the larger whole. Using this simple architectural model, data stored in one location can be much more easily shared between applications. For example, when a patient is registered, demographic information is stored in a database file. The laboratory module from the same system accesses the demographic information from the same database, as do the radiology and pharmacy applications. This sort of collection of applications developed from the same core system can be said to be *integrated* together, in that they are all parts of a single, large system.

In medical centers and large clinics—the targets of this book—that simple architectural model rarely applies to clinical computing systems in use today. There are usually many separately designed computing systems, each contributing a portion of the data and functionality used in clinical care. Medical centers combine data and application functionality from many separate computer systems, some of which may be used by a large number of those involved in patient care, while others may be used by a small number of people specializing in some aspect of care. Instead of sharing a common database, many or all of these smaller applications have their own. To save the cost of re-entering information into each system, and to share data that each system contains, data are exchanged through connections called interfaces. For this reason, this model is referred to as *interfaced* systems.

In most organizations, the clinical computing architecture includes components of both these archetypes: integrated and interfaced systems. There may be a large core system containing integrated applications, and many smaller systems connected to this large system using interfaces. There are other methods that we describe later to permit users to view data originating from separate, smaller systems without realizing they are navigating to other systems.

The organizational clinical computing architecture defines how all the component systems fit together, how they exchange information, standards used within systems and in interfaces, what shared services exist for the benefit of all computing systems, and many other issues [1].

ARCHITECTURE OF COMPUTING SYSTEMS IN HEALTH-CARE ORGANIZATIONS

Since the 1990s, clinical computing system architecture in most large medical centers have followed a similar model. The growth in the number and skill of software vendors has lead to specialization and an explosion of computing options for medical centers to consider. Interface standards have become more widely accepted, as have network standards. What follows is reasonably accurate in most large medical centers and large clinics.

DEPARTMENTAL SYSTEMS

Departmental clinical computing systems are typically selected, and often installed and maintained, by a medical center department such as the clinical laboratory. In the past some clinicians would be given access to departmental systems to look up results, but those working within the department usually use the full features of the departmental system. These are specialized systems, typically developed by companies or talented local experts to meet specialized needs of a medical center department. As computing power and clinician expectation rise, the number and sophistication of departmental systems also rises. Departments lobby, often successfully, to purchase computing systems after seeing them at professional meetings, hearing about them from colleagues, or after searching for an automated solution to growing requirements for data acquisition, analysis, reporting, and research. Specialized vendors are more commonly successful in winning contracts for these systems except for the largest, more complex departments such as pharmacy where vendors who also sell electronic medical record systems may compete successfully. A typical large medical center may have many departmental systems: radiology, cardiology, anatomic pathology, clinical laboratory, gastrointestinal endoscopy, transcription, and many others.

CLINICAL DATA REPOSITORIES

As the number of departmental systems rose, clinicians grew tired of viewing patient results by accessing a separate pharmacy, laboratory, radiology, and other departmental systems. Long ago separate terminals were used for each department resulting in a collection of screens and keyboards on in hospital ward workrooms, each for the purpose of viewing one department's results. Later a single workstation would permit separate applications—each with its own username and password—to be run in its own window. Users would have to learn and remember different user interfaces.

To avoid these problems, and to be able to run rules and queries across data originating in separate departmental systems, the concept of a repository was developed in conjunction with the growth of the database management system industry. A clinical data repository is a database optimized for storage and viewing of clinical information such as laboratory results, transcribed documents, and radiology reports, that is used to store data sent to it over interfaces from departmental systems. A repository permits a clinician to use a web browser or client application to view data originating from a variety of departmental systems. A clinician can now log in once, with a single username and password, to view patient data without memorizing the login process for the laboratory and other departmental systems. Another advantage is that queries and rules to generate reminders can operate in real time across data that originate from a collection of departmental databases. Laboratory results, pharmacy data, demographic information, and allergies can be used in the query running on the clinical data repository, while this would not be possible if the data were only in the departmental system.

BEST OF BREED VERSUS SUITE FROM A SINGLE VENDOR

The phrase "best of breed" refers to the practice of acquiring departmental systems from a wide variety of vendors who offer the best system for each department's needs. Because of vendor specialization, this can result in the medical center having products from many vendors. This practice gained favor in the 1990s along with optimism that interfaces between these systems would solve data exchange needs. Most organizations realize that while selecting the best application from the marketplace had clear advantages for improved functionality, this approach created complexity for users, technical, support, and contracting staff. As we will see in the next chapter, interfaces have clear functional and operational drawbacks and significant costs. As "best of breed" has fallen from favor, there has been resurgence in interest in single-vendor application suites, and compromise with a middle ground in which most applications are from an integrated collection of core systems, with sparing use of specialized department systems.

CORE SYSTEMS

In many medical centers, a single system is often at the center of the organizational clinical computing system architecture. This is often a vendor product, and in fact the organization may be known as a "Vendor X" or "Vendor Y" site because of the selection of that vendor's core product. This may be the system that is used as the core EMR and for CPOE, and may contain the repository. One reason for the growth of core systems is that while creating interfaces between systems has many advantages, there are also drawbacks and limitations to interfaces. They may exchange only a portion of desired information; keeping data synchronized between two or more systems may be very difficult; interfaces are "moving parts" and may fail; they require maintenance and upgrades. And interfaces between some applications such as CPOE and an inpatient pharmacy system are so difficult that many experts recommend they be joined in an integrated core system instead. However, core systems have their own limitations in breadth of functionality. The core system vendor may have an excellent application for some areas but not for others. For this reason and others, departmental systems have grown in number.

NETWORKS, HOSTS, SERVERS, "MIDDLEWARE," WORKSTATIONS

The architecture has many other components beyond the applications themselves. A reliable, secure network is essential to medical centers. The battle for the network protocol is over and TCP/IP has emerged as the choice for nearly all organizations. Wireless networks are quickly becoming something clinicians have grown to expect in medical centers, and play an important role in making bedside rounds and medication administration efficient. For example, if a physician logs in to a wireless device to make rounds it is not necessary to log in at each bedside but merely to select the next patient on the list.

File and application servers are needed to provide storage and small applications essential to the workforce. Other servers may provide decision support applications such as drug interaction databases or clinical event monitors. These applications do not stand on their own, but complement or augment functionality of departmental and core systems, or viewing applications used with the clinical data repository.

Middleware is an older term used when client–server application design was more common. The client application would run on a workstation and concentrate on viewing functions. The server operated in the background to serve the client data in response to request. However, the client and server often weren't enough. A layer of applications between them—called "middleware"—provided mediation between multiple servers and multiple applications, provided caching, and many other functions. Today the terms client–server and middleware are less commonly used.

The choice of workstations and other clinical area devices is very important because of their large number and costs, support costs, and the close connection that users will have to them. The workstation is the most visible and in a sense the most personal part of the clinical computing system. It is also the final pathway through which all systems pass before being used at the bedside or in the clinic.

END-USER APPLICATIONS: STRENGTHS/WEAKNESSES OF WEB AND OTHER DEVELOPMENT CHOICES

The web has revolutionized clinical computing as it has other computing domains. It is ideally suited to presenting data from many sources using a simple, easily learned interface. Web applications run on many operating systems using similar user interface metaphors. They do not need to be distributed, but rather are available wherever needed when the URL is entered. Web development tools have become sophisticated permitting powerful, simple applications that have set the standard for user experience.

Many clinical computing applications are based on the web. It is more commonly used for results reviewing applications, display of PACS images, for remote user and patient access, and as a common front-end to many applications. However, the web has drawbacks that have limited its penetration into all clinical computing applications. Developing sophisticated applications for rapid entry of notes and orders has proved to be very challenging. Some organizations and vendors have stepped back from converting their entire application suite to the web because it was very difficult to provide pop-up windows, alerting, rapidly changing displays, and other features used in traditional client applications. The term Win32 is often applied to applications that run on a windows workstation; Win32 applications are ubiquitous and familiar to all computer users. Many CPOE systems are developed using Win32.

WHAT IS CITRIX? HOW DOES IT WORK?

One of the major disadvantages of Win32 applications is that they usually run in the processor and memory of individual workstation, using a collection of files on the workstation hard drive. Installing any application and its supporting files over thousands of workstations can be very labor intensive. If the applications need to be updated, assuring that all components are updated simultaneously throughout the medical center may require that the computer be restarted, and yet this is not always practical in a busy ICU or ER setting.

To reduce the costs of distributing and maintaining Win32 application to thousands of workstation, an alternative approach has gained favor. Citrix Metaframe can be used to "paint" application screens on the workstation monitor, yet only a small, easily distributed application resides on the workstation, and that application can be distributed over the web. A Citrix server controls what displays on the screen of many— more than a dozen—workstations. The means that updates can be performed on the small number of Citrix servers while the workstations spread throughout the campus. Citrix clients permit Win32 application to run on many operating systems such as Mac OS X and others.

There are disadvantages to the Citrix approach. There are time delays inherent in logging in to an application through a separate layer; the connection between the application running through Citrix and local printers and peripherals may be problematic; screen resolution and windowing may be cumbersome in comparison with running the same application directly on the workstation. Citrix is another layer with risks for failure; in this case failure of a single Citrix server can affect many workstations relying on that server to deliver an important application. Citrix licensing fees are also an important consideration, even when weighed against the additional expense of alternative ways to deliver applications to scattered workstations.

Nevertheless, Citrix is increasingly common in health-care organizations, and is likely to remain an important feature of the architecture of clinical computing systems for a long time.

EXAMPLES OF CLINICAL COMPUTING ARCHITECTURES

Diagrams of clinical computing architectures provide a graphic representation of how the pieces fit together, in varying levels of detail. A classic diagram, first published in MD Computing in 1992 [1] shows departmental systems, a central patient data repository, and shared services such as a dictionary and medical logic modules (Figure 2.1). These are connected using HL7 interfaces and using other mechanisms. This diagram shows one of the earliest architectures using interfaces between systems and a central repository. There were other examples at the time including Boston Children's Hospital and sites supported by National Library of Medicine Integrated Academic Information Management Systems grants. The Veterans Administration was developing clinical and administrative information systems for its facilities based on an integrated, rather than interfaced, approach using the Decentralized Hospital Computing Program [2]. Over time, workstations replaced terminals, imaging and departmental systems

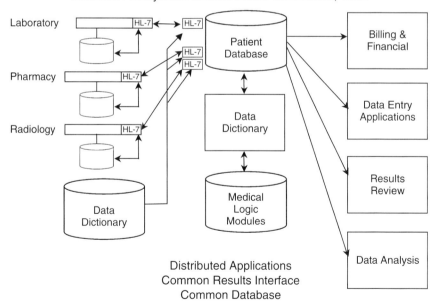

FIGURE 2.1   Architecture of the clinical portion of the CPMC integrated academic information management system. The hybrid architecture comes from multiple interfaced sources, but the results review function is integrated because the users need only gain access to a single patient-oriented database.

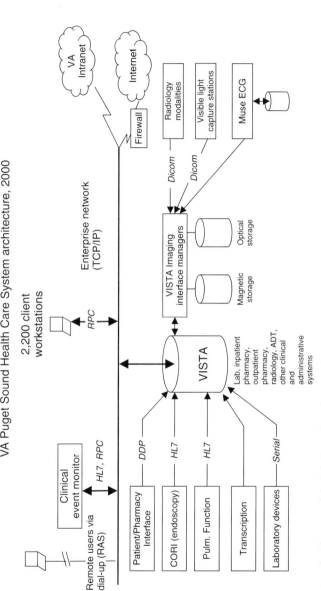

FIGURE 2.2 Architecture of the VA Puget Sound computing system. The foundation is VistA, with contributions by other smaller clinical systems including VistA Imaging and departmental systems. RPC = Remote Procedure Call; Dicom = Digital Communications in Medicine; HL7 = Health Level 7; VistA = Veterans Integrated System Technical Architecture.

UW Medicine clinical computing architecture, 2006

UW Medicine
Information Technology Services (ITS)
ORCA – Electronic Medical Record
Data Flow Diagram for Phase I

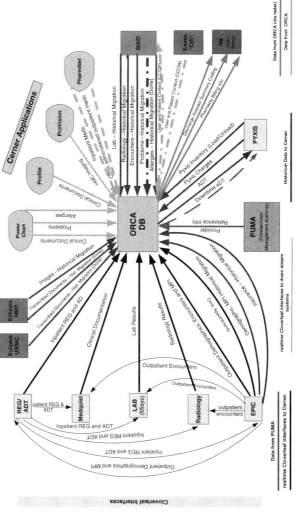

FIGURE 2.3 This diagram shows relationship between multiple core systems (Cerner, referred to as ORCA in this diagram, Epic, and MIND), departmental systems (Misys laboratory, IDX laboratory, Emtek (now Eclipsys) bedside documentation, Pyxis medication dispensing system, and the many interfaces that connect them using the Cloverleaf interface engine and other mechanisms. Not shown are many other departmental systems (Tamtron anatomic pathology, Muse ECG, GE PACS, and others), smaller servers, and workstations.

were added to the core MUMPS-based DHCP, and the VA reflected this by changing the name for their architecture to VistA, which stands for Veterans Integrated Systems Technical Architecture. A diagram of the architecture of one VA medical center is shown in Figure 2.2. In this example, the core VA software, derived from DHCP, is only part of a broader system which includes a TCP/IP network, departmental systems, and workstations.

A diagram of the UW Medicine system architecture (Figure 2.3) shows some of the many departmental systems connected by an extensive network using a commercial interface engine and several core systems by a variety of commercial vendors. The complexity of this system is apparent, and is rising as more components are added each year. The challenge of maintaining and improving the infrastructure that supports this architecture is an important theme of this book.

The architecture of nearly all medical centers and large clinics includes interfaces which are of critical importance for data exchange, coordination of demographic information, and many other purposes. Because of the value and problems associated with interfaces, we turn to this subject next.

REFERENCES

[1] Clayton PD, Sideli RV, and Sengupta, S. Open architecture and integrated information at Columbia-Presbyterian Medical Center.,MD Comput. 1992; 9: 297–303.
[2] Kolodner RM (ed.) Computerizing Large Integrated Health Networks: The VA Success New York: Springer-Verlag, 1997.

3

CREATING AND SUPPORTING

INTERFACES

THOMAS PAYNE

*IT Services, UW Medicine, Departments of Medicine, Health Services,
and Medical Education & Biomedical Informatics, University of Washington,
Seattle, WA*

JAMES HOATH

UW Medicine, Seattle, WA

For those interested in clinical computing operations, understanding what interfaces between clinical computing systems are and how they work is extremely important. Many of the key features of clinical computing systems, such as gathering data about one or many patients into a single view, are dependent on interfaces. Many unrealistic claims by vendors and hopeful clinicians and organizational leaders can be traced to a misunderstanding of what interface technology can accomplish and its costs. Because so many vendor claims of seamless operation of their products depend on flawlessly operating interfaces that, only partly in jest, we have subtitled this chapter "Interfaces in the real world: What you won't learn at HIMSS."

INTEGRATING AND INTERFACING APPLICATIONS

WHAT DO WE MEAN BY INTEGRATION?

Webster's defines integrates as "to form, coordinate, or blend into a functioning or unified whole." In clinical computing, integration means to bring together data and functions so that users operate as though there is one application satisfying their patient information and application needs. Behind the scenes, the data originate from different physical and virtual locations, on different systems. How can we provide users with the integrated view they seek?

TECHNIQUES TO ACHIEVE THIS

There are a variety of ways to provide this integration. One way, as we have seen previously, is to actually have all needed data in a single location and all applications based on the same system. As we have also seen, this is much less likely to occur because of growth of specialized departmental and special function applications. An alternative approach is to develop a web front-end that collects data from disparate applications but displays it on the web viewer as though the data originate from a single source. A third, and the most common way, is to collect a copy of data from disparate departmental systems using a connection over the network between different systems, using data exchange protocols and data standards. This is what we mean by an interface.

HL7 IN THE REAL WORLD

INTEGRATION BEFORE HL7

Before the advent of data exchange standards, every interface between clinical systems was completely customized and consequently very expensive. It required that experts in the two systems to be interfaced agree upon data exchange standards and the form in which their data were to be exchanged. After agreement was achieved, each would write an application on the sending and receiving system to permit data exchange. The high cost of this effort reduced the number of interfaces that could be developed. This cost motivated industry and researchers to create standards to be used in creating interfaces. Partly based on the work of Donald Simborg at UCSF, a data exchange protocol came into use, and standards to represent the data themselves were also developed. The data exchange standard became Health Level 7, known as HL7. Data standards were created largely by standards organizations such as the American Society for Testing and Materials (ASTM), some of which were subsumed by HL7.

WHAT HL7 STANDS FOR

The International Organization for Standardization (ISO) developed a seven-layer model for communications across a network as part of the open systems interconnection (OSI) initiative. Each of the seven layers represented a different component:

Layer 7: Application layer
Layer 6: Presentation layer
Layer 5: Session layer
Layer 4: Transport layer
Layer 3: Network layer
Layer 2: Data Link layer
Layer 1: Physical layer

Health Level 7 takes its name from the seventh layer and is devoted to standards to simplify health-care data exchange. The term HL7 now applies both to the standard and to a standards developing organization that produces the standard.

HL7 DEFINITION, HISTORY, AND EVOLUTION

HL7 has had multiple versions, starting with version 1 and now at version 3. It is version 2, however, that is used in the vast majority of medical centers worldwide. The HL7 standard is a printed document divided into many chapters (Figure 3.1). Each chapter describes how data of a different type are to be created in messages or "event types" (Figure 3.2). In general, data are placed in segments of a long string of ASCII printable characters where the

■ **Version 2.x**

Patient Administration – Admit, Discharge, Transfer, and Demographics.

Order Entry – Orders for Clinical Services and Observations, Pharmacy, Dietary, and Supplies.

Query – Rules applying to queries and to their responses.

Financial Management – Patient Accounting and Charges.

Observation Reporting – Observation Report Messages.

Master Files – Health Care Application Master Files.

Medical Records/Information Management – Document Management Services and Resources.

Scheduling – Appointment Scheduling and Resources.

Patient Referral – Primary Care Referral Messages.

Patient Care – Problem-Oriented Records.

Laboratory – Automation Equipment status, specimen status, equipment inventory, equipment comment, equipment response, equipment notification, equipment test code settings, equipment logs/service.

Application Management – Application control-level requests, transmission of application management information.

Personnel Management – Professional affiliations, educational details, language detail, practitioner organization unit, practitioner detail, staff identification.

FIGURE 3.1   The HL7 2.x standard is grouped into a defined set of functional areas such as Patient Administration, Order Entry, and others shown here.

- ADMIT/VISITNOTIFICATION (EVENT A01)
- TRANSFER A PATIENT (EVENT A02)
- DISCHARGE/END VISIT (EVENT A03)
- REGISTER A PATIENT (EVENT A04)
- PRE-ADMIT A PATIENT (EVENT A05)
- CHANGE AN OUTPATIENT TO AN INPATIENT (EVENT A06)
- CHANGE AN INPATIENT TO AN OUTPATIENT (EVENT A07)
- UPDATE PATIENT INFORMATION (EVENT A08)
- PATIENT DEPARTING – TRACKING (EVENT A09)
- PATIENT ARRIVING – TRACKING (EVENT A10)
- CANCEL ADMIT / VISIT NOTIFICATION (EVENT A11)
- CANCEL TRANSFER (EVENT A12)
- CANCEL DISCHARGE / END VISIT (EVENT A13)
- PENDING ADMIT (EVENT A14)
- PENDING TRANSFER (EVENT A15)
- PENDING DISCHARGE (EVENT A16)
- SWAP PATIENTS (EVENT A17)
- MERGE PATIENT INFORMATION (EVENT A18)
- PATIENT QUERY (EVENT A19)
- BED STATUS UPDATE (EVENT A20)
- PATIENT GOES ON A LEAVE OF ABSENCE (EVENT A21)
- PATIENT RETURNS FROM A LEAVE OF ABSENCE (EVENT A22)
- DELETE A PATIENT RECORD (EVENT A23)
- LINK PATIENT INFORMATION (EVENT A24)
- CANCEL PENDING DISCHARGE (EVENT A25)
- CANCEL PENDING TRANSFER (EVENT A26)
- CANCEL PENDING ADMIT (EVENT A27)
- ADD PERSON OR PATIENT INFORMATION (EVENT A28)
- DELETE PERSON INFORMATION (EVENT A29)
- MERGE PERSON INFORMATION (EVENT A30)
- UPDATE PERSON INFORMATION (EVENT A31)
- CANCEL PATIENT ARRIVING – TRACKING (EVENT A32)
- CANCEL PATIENT DEPARTING – TRACKING (EVENT A33)
- MERGE PATIENT INFORMATION – PATIENT ID ONLY (EVENT A34)
- MERGE PATIENT INFORMATION – ACCOUNT NUMBER ONLY (EVENT A35)
- MERGE PATIENT INFORMATION – PATIENT ID & ACCOUNT NUMBER (EVENT A36)
- UNLINK PATIENT INFORMATION (EVENT A37)
- CANCEL PRE-ADMIT (EVENT A38)
- MERGE PERSON – PATIENT ID (EVENT A39)
- MERGE PATIENT – PATIENT IDENTIFIER LIST (EVENT A40)
- MERGE ACCOUNT – PATIENT ACCOUNT NUMBER (EVENT A41)
- MERGE VISIT – VISIT NUMBER (EVENT A42)
- MOVE PATIENT INFORMATION – PATIENT IDENTIFIER LIST (EVENT A43)
- MOVE ACCOUNT INFORMATION – PATIENT ACCOUNT NUMBER (EVENT A44)
- MOVE VISIT INFORMATION – VISIT NUMBER (EVENT A45)
- CHANGE PATIENT ID (EVENT A46)
- CHANGE PATIENT IDENTIFIER LIST (EVENT A47)
- CHANGE ALTERNATE PATIENT ID (EVENT A48)
- CHANGE PATIENT ACCOUNT NUMBER (EVENT A49)
- CHANGE VISIT NUMBER (EVENT A50)
- CHANGE ALTERNATE VISIT ID (EVENT A51)
- CANCEL LEAVE OF ABSENCE FOR A PATIENT (EVENT A52)
- CANCEL PATIENT RETURNS FROM A LEAVE OF ABSENCE (EVENT A53)
- CHANGE ATTENDING DOCTOR (EVENT A54)
- CANCEL CHANGE ATTENDING DOCTOR (EVENT A55)
- GET PERSON DEMOGRAPHICS (QBP) AND RESPONSE (RSP) (EVENTS Q21 AND K21)
- FIND CANDIDATES (QBP) AND RESPONSE (RSP) (EVENTS Q22 AND K22)
- GET CORRESPONDING IDENTIFIERS (QBP) AND RESPONSE (RSP) (EVENTS Q23 AND K23)
- ALLOCATE IDENTIFIERS (QBP) AND RESPONSE (RSP) (EVENTS Q24 AND K24)
- UPDATE ADVERSE REACTION INFORMATION (EVENT A60)
- CHANGE CONSULTING DOCTOR (EVENT A61)
- CANCEL CHANGE CONSULTING DOCTOR (EVENT A62)

FIGURE 3.2   Each functional area has its own set of defined Message types (Event types). For example, these are the message types from the Admission Discharge Transfer (ADT) functional area.

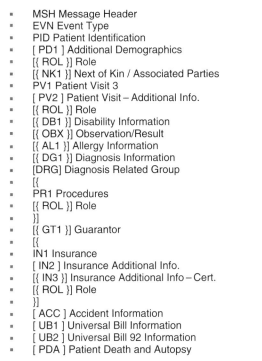

- MSH Message Header
- EVN Event Type
- PID Patient Identification
- [PD1] Additional Demographics
- [{ ROL }] Role
- [{ NK1 }] Next of Kin / Associated Parties
- PV1 Patient Visit 3
- [PV2] Patient Visit – Additional Info.
- [{ ROL }] Role
- [{ DB1 }] Disability Information
- [{ OBX }] Observation/Result
- [{ AL1 }] Allergy Information
- [{ DG1 }] Diagnosis Information
- [DRG] Diagnosis Related Group
- [{
- PR1 Procedures
- [{ ROL }] Role
- }]
- [{ GT1 }] Guarantor
- [{
- IN1 Insurance
- [IN2] Insurance Additional Info.
- [{ IN3 }] Insurance Additional Info – Cert.
- [{ ROL }] Role
- }]
- [ACC] Accident Information
- [UB1] Universal Bill Information
- [UB2] Universal Bill 92 Information
- [PDA] Patient Death and Autopsy

FIGURE 3.3   Positional syntax. An HL7 message is composed of a set of defined segments. As an example, an Admission message (A01) is composed of the segments shown here.

position of the data element determines its meaning according to the HL7 protocol (Figure 3.3). Data contained within various positions within the message can be represented according to codes from HL7 or other standards. HL7 messages are the conveyance; the contents of the message vary and must be agreed to by both the sending and receiving systems in Version 2.

HL7 version 3 is a departure from previous versions and is not broadly adopted. It is based on a reference information model (RIM) that is an essential part of the standard. Organizations using HL7 version 3 adopt the RIM to represent the data within the message.

HL7 COMMUNICATION PROTOCOLS

HL7 contains more than just the data to be exchanged. It also handles message acknowledgment, and other features. It can also be used to "encapsulate" data such as representations of images and other images. HL7 does not insist on TCP/IP for use but this protocol has become the health-care industry standard.

WHAT IS NEEDED TO SUCCEED WITH
INTERFACE DEVELOPMENT?

A common misconception is that if two clinical computing systems are "HL7 compatible" that creating an interface is only slightly more difficult than plugging in the power cord of an appliance, or connecting a network cable to a computer. The reality is that though interface creation is much simpler than without use of HL7, it remains difficult, expensive, and time-consuming.

FOUNDATION

Interfaces are substantially simpler if they are created on a firm organizational foundation. The foundation can include a common data model among the core applications so that data such as patient names and identifiers can be incorporated into messages the same way for many interfaces. There may be a standardized master file, which is itself kept in synchrony with departmental and core applications within the organization. This master file can include data such as payors, locations, providers, and other commonly used information.

INTERFACE ENGINES

Interface engines are one of the most important technologies to be applied to clinical computing over the last 20 years. They are essentially application level routers, or "traffic cops," that serve as a central hub for HL7 message exchange. Interface engines are actually complex applications that run on powerful hardware, and are key components of interfaces in most medical centers.

The purpose of an interface engine is to reduce the number of interfaces that need to be coded and supported, and to make interfaces more reliable. If there are four systems that need to share information using an interface, then one option is to build an interface between each pair of the four systems. The number of interfaces needed can be expressed by the formula

$$\frac{n(n-1)}{2}$$

Or in the case of four systems, there need to be six interfaces. If there are eight systems, the number of point-to-point systems is 28. This number would be extremely difficult both to create and to maintain. An alternative is to have a central hub for the interfaces, connected to each system. Any message could pass to the hub and be routed to the destination system through that system's interface to the hub. In this model there are only four interfaces for four systems, and eight interfaces for eight systems. The central hub is the interface engine, and it can greatly reduce effort required to build interfaces in an organization (Figures 3.4 and 3.5).

They also allow the enterprise to purchase the "vanilla" product and maintain control over needed customization internally. This reduces purchase and maintenance costs as well as simplifies the

Why use an Interface Engine?

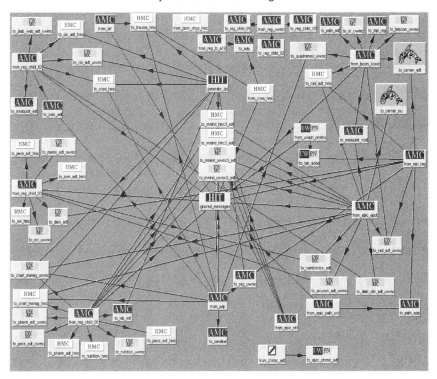

Point to Point Architecture

FIGURE 3.4   This figure illustrates the number of point-to-point interfaces required to connect the UW Medicine clinical computing systems if an interface engine were not used. Each arrow represents a separate HL7 interface. In reality, these point-to-point interfaces are not used. Figure 3.5 shows how this is accomplished with an interface engine.

Why use an Interface Engine?

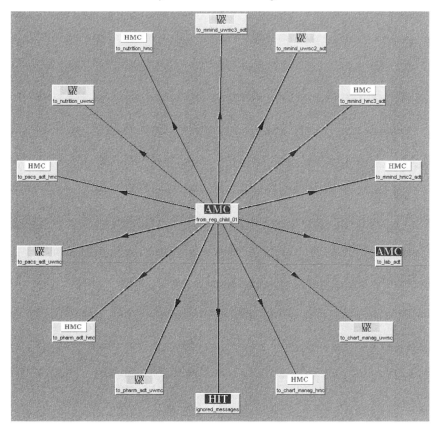

Engine architecture

FIGURE 3.5   This figure shows how an interface engine can reduce the number of interfaces required to connect separate systems (symbolized by rectangles). A smaller number of interfaces connects each system to the interface engine, which then routes messages from the originating system to systems to which the messages are to be sent.

process of upgrading applications because there is no custom code that must also be upgraded.

There are other functions that an interface engine can serve, some of which are commonly used, and others of which are more controversial. It can provide routing as discussed above, node management, documentation of interfaces, interface monitoring, and notification of interface status and signs of problems. It can also be used for other purposes that are controversial because of their potential to introduce problems: Moving data from field to field, look-ups, invasive filtering, and full-blown data invention.

INTERFACE DEVELOPMENT

Why is interface development so difficult? At its core, it is not different than other software development. It is quite complex because of the number of factors involved: two different systems sending and receiving large amounts of data, some of which may not be anticipated. It requires careful analysis with strong under-standing of the source and destination system. One small change in the source system can potentially affect a large number of destination systems.

INTERFACE DEVELOPMENT METHODOLOGY

This includes analysis, an understanding of workflow (current and future state), specification gap analysis, technical specification devel-opment, coding, testing, and finally implementation.

WHY ISN'T DEVELOPING AN HL7 INTERFACE EASIER?

In some organizations including our own, there is a lack some fundamentals:

- Major differences in core system data models and the ramifications (encounter-based vs. MRN-based with no corollary for encounter model).
- There may be no master file standardization (for example, a provider list).

In addition, all vendors implement HL7 slightly differently. This leads to the aphorism, "Once you have developed one HL7 interface, you have developed one HL7 interface."

Interface development is costly, both in time and budget. At the University of Washington an HL7 interface may take 6 months to create. The literature suggests that the cost for a single interface may be $50 000 [1]; at UW we sometimes budget $150 000 per interface.

When installing a new clinical computing system, the required and desired interfaces (from ADT, results out to the repository, orders to be transmitted to the system) may exceed the cost of the system itself.

Once created, interfaces need maintenance, they fail (for example, because the interface engine fails, or the sending or receiving system or network connection fails), and they need replacement if one of the sending or receiving systems is replaced or undergoes an extensive upgrade.

OTHER STANDARDS

There are many other standards used within health-care organizations and methods to bring data and functionality together, which are described in detail elsewhere [2, 3].

X12

This standard is used primarily for financial transactions.

DICOM

DICOM stands for Digital Communications in Medicine, and is one of the most successfully applied standards in clinical computing. It is used for the exchange of image data between PACS and other systems. The imaging vendor community along with standards development organizations collaborated to create DICOM.

CCOW

CCOW stands for Clinical Context Object Workgroup, and has a more current name within its parent organization, The Clinical Context Management Specification. It permits compliant applications to share context, patient and encounter selection, and in general to operate together on the same workstation, as though they were part of the same application.

ARDEN SYNTAX

Arden Syntax was developed as an outgrowth of a retreat at the Arden Homestead in New York state. The purpose of the retreat was to find ways to share decision support modules between different clinical computing systems. There was great enthusiasm initially, but adoption of Arden Syntax has been lower than initially envisioned. The pioneering work that lead to the development of this standard has aided efforts to share encoded knowledge.

FINAL THOUGHTS REGARDING INTERFACES

Complex and diverse workflow in health-care delivery results in pressures for computing systems to be developed or tailored to needs of specialties. The needs of an orthopedic and cardiology practice are different; it is not surprising, therefore, that the two groups see advantage to having a computing system tailored for them. This can result in many different clinical computing systems within the organization, each with its own login and password, list of authorized users, user interface, and most importantly its specialty data about a patient's health. One solution is to make the system difference transparent to clinicians either by exchanging data through an interface or by creating a view in one system that contains data in the departmental system. However, these tasks take time and resources and the growth in the number of specialized systems may exceed the organization's ability to create new interfaces and views. The result is that introducing the new system may create simpler workflow and contribute valuable data to the specialist, but the general clinical user will face more complexity: One more place to remember to access, or to ask the department to send data. In the press of busy practice, often the dedicated time to search for data in myriad locations is deemed less important than other tasks, and important data are missed. We know that clinicians are accustomed to making decisions with incomplete data.

Vendors who supply clinical computing system to health-care organizations are generally paid in two ways: Licensing fees and maintenance contracts, both applied to software their firm creates and supports. Integrating systems from different vendors so that clinicians can find information easily is almost always the responsibility of the organization itself. Vendors point out that the need for interfaces is reduced if more applications are licensed from them rather than purchased from different vendors, and if an interface is needed, they have created HL7 interfaces with many other vendors. The cost of creating HL7 interfaces is considerable—estimated at

$50 000 per interface but higher than this in UW experience, typically requiring a year or more from plan to production use. So the vendor promise of HL7 interfaces solving the problem of dispersion of clinical information is expensive, time-consuming, and often unfulfilled. The majority of the burden falls on the organization and not on the vendor.

REFERENCES

[1] Walker J, Pan E, Johnston D, et al. The value of health care information exchange and interoperability. Health Aff (Millwood). 2005 Jan-Jun; Suppl Web Exclusives: W5-10-W5-18.
[2] Huff SM. Clinical data exchange standards and vocabularies for messages. Proc AMIA Symp. 1998; 62–7.
[3] Norris T, Fuller S, Goldberg H, and Tarczy-Hornoch P (eds) Informatics for Primary Care. New York: Springer-Verlag, 2002.

4

INFRASTRUCTURE AND SECURITY

DAVID CHOU

Department of Laboratory Medicine, University of Washington, Seattle, WA

SOUMITRA SENGUPTA

Department of Biomedical Informatics, Columbia University, New York, NY

INTRODUCTION

Infrastructure refers to those resources and items required to successfully support and operate information systems. These items include, but are not limited to, security, networks, computers and closely associated hardware, their operation and management, computer rooms, and desktop computers. Many of these resources may be purchased from an outside vendor, or these services can be budgeted for and provided by groups within an organization. Often infrastructure items require large capital expenditures, lengthy lead times, and highly technical skills.

Security refers to policies, procedures, software, and/or hardware designed to insure that data in information systems are protected against accidental or inappropriate destruction, alteration, or access. Proper management of security requires attention to both infrastructure and information system designs, as well as the organization adhering to strict and appropriate personnel practices. Security should not be viewed as comprehensive and complete. Indeed, comprehensive security approach may be so detailed and expensive that it will fail to achieve its goals. An approach that evaluates risks and defends only the most significant risks may be far more effective.

Both infrastructure and security are among the many invisible processes and resources required to implement and sustain a successful clinical computing system. Some resources, such as a data center, must be available prior to implementation of these systems; many other resources, such as those supporting security, should be available prior to implementation, but are often deferred until problems occur. Most infrastructure requirements continue and expand after the system is in use.

DATA CENTERS (COMPUTER ROOMS)

Historically, mainframe computers, with the need for a controlled physical environment including temperature, electrical power, and humidity, have been housed in dedicated and protected facilities. These facilities are often referred to as *data centers* or *computer rooms*. As computers shrunk in size and power, many migrated from expensive data centers into the business office or factory floor. The data center is reemerging in importance; however, as computer systems start handling mission critical services such as the monitoring of critical business functions and operations, as computer densities begin to tax the usual office environment, and as networked computers require protection from malicious Internet attacks.

Most computers used in a data center are mounted in an industry standard cabinet, referred to as a *rack*. Racks are approximately 2 feet wide, 3 feet deep, and 6 feet high. Rack mounted computers are bolted horizontally into a rack, with units stacked above each other like a pancake. All rack mounted computers are 19″ wide and range up to 36″ deep. The amount of vertical space or height occupied by a computer varies. The height of a computer is measured in multiples of 1.75″ and each 1.75″ is referred to as a "RU" (for rack unit). Thus a 2RU computer will occupy 3.5″ of vertical space in a rack. A full rack supports 42RU of equipment. Rack mounted computers are available as small as 1RU, and those larger than 7RU are uncommon. An RU may also be abbreviated as U.

As with any construction project, building a new data center requires lengthy lead times. In addition to the usual construction requirements, data centers have large demands for electricity, cooling, and backup electrical generators and their fuel tanks, all of which require special arrangements and/or permits. With growth in use of

Computers in a rack. Each unit is 2RU.

computers in healthcare and business, the demand for data center facilities has skyrocketed with predictable consequences in both construction costs for a new data center and leasing costs for commercial data centers. Total construction costs for data center in 2007 in an urban area can range from $2000 to over $6000 per square foot, or at least an order of magnitude more than that for conventional office space. Leased space is usually charged by the rack, with costs of $1000–2000/rack/month common in urban areas.

ELECTRICAL POWER

Modern computers use lots of electricity. As we will see, providing enough electricity and cooling is now a critical part of clinical computing operations. The amount of electricity consumed is measured in watts. A desktop computer consumes 200–500 watts while the larger server computer in a data center consumes 250–1000 watts. Larger units of measure include the kilowatt or 1000 watts and the megawatt or 1 000 000 watts. A kilowatt is the amount of electricity used by a medium sized refrigerator; 20 kilowatts is the amount of electricity used by a home. Power consumption is measured in kilowatt hours (kwh) or the consumption of 1 kilowatt for one hour. One kwh costs under $0.02 for hydro generated commercial power and is as high as $0.25 in urban areas. Computers in an institution with thousands of computers can consume megawatts of power.

Assuming that all electrical energy used by a computer is converted to heat (in reality very little of a computer's electricity is converted to light or motion), 3.414 British thermal units (BTUs) of heat is produced for each watt. One BTU is the amount of energy used to heat 1 gallon of water 1°F. Thus, a 1000 watt system will generate 3414 BTUs of heat. Cooling is commonly measured in tons, an arcane unit related to a ton of ice once used for refrigeration. At the conversion rate of 12 000 BTUs/ton of cooling, about three to four 1000 watt computers can be cooled by a one-ton air conditioner. A 3–6 ton air conditioner cools a typical home.

Power and cooling limit the number of computers in a data center rather than space. Here is why: a full rack supporting 42-1RU computers consumes more than 20 kilowatts of electricity, produces over 68 000 BTUs of heat, and requires almost 6 tons of cooling. If 100 such racks were placed in a 4000 square foot room, 600 tons of cooling and 2 megawatts of electricity would be required, or 500 watts of electricity per square foot. Modern homes and offices are designed for electrical power densities of 10 watts/square foot. Using conventional construction, most computer rooms are designed for power densities up to 150 watts/square foot. In the 1970s, most computer rooms operated at 40 watts/square foot. Cooling a room with a power density of 500 watts/square foot is not easy using conventional air cooling. With conventional air cooling, most facilities can only service densities of 6 kilowatts/rack to insure that there is sufficient cooling.

Electrical requirements for a data center have become enormous. Data centers require electricity for both computers and cooling. In a typical installation, the amount of power needed to cool a room is approximately equal to that required to run the computers. Even a moderate 20 000 square foot data centers will consume megawatts of power, exceeding the power used by most moderate sized office buildings. For high density data centers, the electrical costs are significant. For example, a data center consuming 2 megawatts running 24 hours a day will spend over $1.75 million/year on electricity at $0.10/kw hour. No wonder that Internet companies have located data centers in the Pacific Northwest where inexpensive hydroelectric power is available. When building a data center, the large electrical loads may also require electrical considerations not normally expected in usual construction. For example, transformers, switches, and wiring subsystems must have enough capacity to handle the additional electrical load. If a local power substation serving the region is operating near capacity limits, it may also require upgrades and these costs may be passed back. In such cases, any building and substation upgrades will be costly.

POWER DISTRIBUTION AND BACKUP POWER

The large amount of power being handled in a data center requires careful attention to the distribution of power. Typically power entering a data center is distributed through circuit breakers in electrical panels and power distribution units (PDUs). PDUs distribute power to racks through flexible wiring systems. Momentary power outages can cause computers to corrupt data. Therefore, data centers also include some form of systems to protect against power outages. For periods up to 30 minutes, uninterruptible power supplies (UPS) supply power from storage batteries, which are usually lead acid batteries similar to what are found in cars. Facilities requiring protection against longer electrical outages install backup generators, which are limited only by available fuel. Generators require several minutes to start, so a UPS is required with generators. Both generators and UPSs are expensive to install and maintain. UPS batteries must be replaced at 3–5-year intervals. Generators must be tested under a power load on a periodic basis, often disrupting normal computer operations. Even fuel must be flushed on a periodic basis, so facilities with large supplies bear the cost of rising diesel costs. A facility should examine its power outage patterns to determine the type of backup power systems required. To reduce expenses, the facility can limit backup power to only critical systems.

COOLING

Dense computer racks generate heat and challenges for cooling. Even with satisfactory ambient temperatures in the computer room, internal temperatures inside the computer can exceed acceptable operating parameters. For example, Intel specifies that the Pentium 4 chip must operate under 40°C (104°F). If a room temperature of 78°F results in a rack temperature of 95°F because of poor circulation or a fan failure, the chip temperature will easily exceed this.

Traditional computer rooms have used a *raised floor* to carry cold air to computers. The raised floor also acts as a raceway for electrical power and wiring connecting computers. Openings in removable floor panels allow cold air to emerge near heat sources. Raised floors can range from 12–18″ deep for a medium density computer room to 4 feet or more for a high density computer room. Hot air is exhausted through ceiling ducts or plenums. Plenums are often enclosed raised ceilings used for heating/ventilating/air-conditioning and for cables, piping, and lighting. Some data center designs provide cooling, exhaust, and wiring with cable trays and ducts hanging from the ceiling using this plenum space. This approach eliminates the cost of a raised floor and can be equally effective.

Both raised floor and ceiling designs arrange equipment racks in rows. Corridors between racks alternate between cold rows, where chilled air is dumped, or hot rows, where computers exhaust heated air. Rack mounted computers are designed to suck air from the front of the rack and exhaust to the back of the rack. Typically, refrigeration units cool water to 40°F. This water is then pumped to heat exchangers in the data center where the water cools the air. Recent energy conservation laws often require that cooling uses outside air when temperatures drop below 40°F instead of refrigeration (using "economizers"). Cooling may be limited by refrigeration capacity as well as the physical limits of plenums to deliver air and plumbing to deliver water.

Power and cooling have become major constraints in the design of data centers because of both expense and complexity. Computer demands for most hospitals have grown significantly in the last decade and will likely continue. An organization must anticipate requirements for data centers and resource them accordingly years in advance of needs. If such projections are not made, projects will either suffer delays associated with the building of new data centers or will require large expenditures leasing space from commercial suppliers or both.

WEIGHT

Data centers face challenges beyond power and cooling. Fully loaded racks are heavy. If a 1RU computer weights 50 pounds, a 42RU rack

Two rows of racks in a data center.

loaded with computers will weigh over 2000 pounds (a ton!), or 200 pounds/square foot if the rack is distributed over 10 square feet. This exceeds the capacity of many building structures. Required and heavy supporting equipment, such as air conditioners, power transformers, batteries, and generators, add to the weight problem. Water cooling and more sophisticated cooling methods such as chilled Freon bathing allow computer densities to increase further and increase the weight problem. Construction of single floor structures, of course, can eliminate weight issues by allowing all equipment to be on the ground where weight limits are largely unlimited. Unfortunately, this imposes large space requirements and may not be practical in dense urban areas.

DATA CENTER RELIABILITY

An industry organization (The Uptime Institute, http://www.uptimeinsitute.com) has categorized data center reliability for power, cooling, and data networks into Tiers 1 through 4, where Tier 1 is a basic facility and Tier 4 is the most reliable [1]. This reliability ranking is useful for describing a facility, but does not address common computer system failures due to human, hardware, and software factors. Data center reliability is one of many factors influencing robustness of information systems, their ability to recover from a disaster, and in providing business continuity after a mishap. These additional areas will be covered later.

A Tier 1 facility does not have any redundancy in air-conditioning, power, or networking, so any failure or maintenance of a single component will result in the loss of operations. A Tier 2 facility provides $n + 1$ redundancy where extra devices can cover any single failure. For example, if four air-conditioning units are required, a fifth unit will be available for operation. Should one of the units fail or require maintenance, the extra unit is placed into service. UPS and generators are required to protect against power loss. Routine maintenance requires annual downtime. A Tier 3 computer room is similar, but does not require downtime for maintenance. A Tier 4 facility is fully fault tolerant, e.g., there are at least two independent sources of power, cooling, and data networks and no single infrastructure failure or maintenance event will cause the computer room to shut down. Construction costs typically increase 30–50% with each tier. The building costs of a basic Tier 1 computer facility in a densely populated urban area including power, cooling, and data networks can exceed $1000 per square foot.

DATA CENTER MANAGEMENT AND REMOTE DATA CENTERS

As is true for any other resource, data centers require people for their management and operation. Someone must perform short- and long-term planning, staging and initial setup of the data center, and day-to-day data center operations. Should an organization decide to build their own data center, it should expect lead times of 2 years or more. Architectural design, property acquisition, budgeting, construction permits, and electric utility access can lengthen this time. Data center design usually requires special skills not usually possessed by healthcare organizations, so consultants or outside firms must be engaged.

Most organizations will, at least in part, depend on the use of commercial data center facilities. These are typically more expensive than building a local on-site facility, but are available more rapidly. However, even leasing commercial facilities may require months, and most facilities require the user to provide some additional equipment. Because of these lead times, organizations must anticipate and plan for data centers, computers, and other equipment needed to service them. Data center capacity planning should take into consideration any equipment undergoing a replacement cycle. For example, computers replaced on a 5-year cycle imply that funding must be available to replace 20% of an organization's systems. Systems undergoing replacement or refreshing will require both old and new systems to be operating simultaneously during conversion and testing. Therefore, an additional 20% in data center capacity will be required in a steady state. The time required for data center planning may be minimal, such as in an organization with an effective 5-year capital equipment planning process where equipment replacement is scheduled, or highly chaotic in one where new equipment appears on short notice, requiring rapid negotiation of leases and the use of contract personnel for installations.

Staging of equipment into a data center requires a second set of skills. Before computer equipment can be placed into a data center, preparatory work may be needed, some by the facility and some by the system owner. The leaser will provide his own equipment racks, or the new equipment may come with its own racks. These need to be moved into the data center, assembled, and connected to power and network. Typically, primary electrical and network connections are provided by the facility. The user may be expected to provide one's own UPS, and the Internet connection may require a firewall and other network devices before computers can be connected. Those outfitting and setting up the data center should also be responsible for documenting the details of the installation should repair or changes be needed.

Once in use, day-to-day operation of computer systems are transferred to staff trained for a structured set of responsibilities. This operation typically handles routine activities such as the managing of system backups, reviewing error logs, checking for environmental alarms and other problems, and handling emergencies. Computers are sufficiently reliable that most activities, including those for environmental alarms, computer consoles, and many others can be handled remotely. These unattended computer rooms are referred to

Data center wiring is time consuming. Attention is required to maintain order.

as "lights-out" data centers. The direct operating expenses for an unattended data center may be lower, but the time for problem detection and resolution are likely to be increased. If software suffers frequent failures, an unattended data center overall may be more expensive.

Systems automating data centers and high speed networks have become so effective that many organizations have moved their facilities from expensive urban locations to less expensive rural areas. When properly located, both facility and electrical costs are lower. Remote data centers can also act as a backup site. Remote data centers, however, trade off decreased costs with the following: (1) Substantial personnel time can be lost to travel when systems require staging or repair. (2) Personnel cannot respond rapidly to problems unless there are duplicate staff at the remote site. (3) Remote data centers are vulnerable to loss of network connectivity during disasters—a common problem in recent disasters—rendering them unusable by the health-care facility they serve.

FUTURE OF DATA CENTERS

Because of their expense, considerable attention has been given toward reducing the growth of data centers. These include better chip designs, more efficient computers, and software designed to increase the utilization of lightly used systems.

Successive generations of chip designs have reduced hardware power consumption relative to performance, but newer operating and applications software have consumed much of this improvement. This historical precedent will likely continue, and the demand for CPU cycles seems insatiable. Intel has demonstrated an integrated circuit with 80 individual CPUs on a single chip consuming 65 watts, an unusually low power requirement for a chip of this complexity. Software has been evolving toward ever larger and increasingly complex applications. Meanwhile, applications such as EMRs tax even the largest hardware implementations available today. Hardware vendors are delivering newer systems with reduced power consumption. Computers can vary by three fold or more in their power requirements, largely dictated by their computational capacity. Selecting a power conserving computer may sacrifice computational performance, so such hardware may not be appropriate for all applications.

Virtualization is software and/or hardware which permit multiple copies of an operating system and associated applications to run on a single computer. Such software can reduce hardware requirements for systems with low utilization such as those used for testing or training. This additional layer can reduce hardware at the expense of increased complexity for maintenance and testing and may not be compatible with all software. As integrated circuits designed with multiple cores increase in availability (i.e., multiple cores increase the number of processors on the same chip), virtualization will become more common to make effective use of the chip.

The delays and costs to finance, design, and build a data center present challenges to many organizations. To meet the need for rapid deployment of a data center, one hardware vendor has introduced a 20″ by 8″ self-contained shipping container designed to house more than 230RU's of computers (project Black Box, http://www.sun. com). Such a data center can be shipped by truck or other common carrier following a disaster or to meet an urgent need, but still requires the user address to provide 60 tons of cooling, 200 kilowatts of power for the hardware plus an equal amount for cooling and network connections. Compared to traditional construction, this option also appears to less expensive and presents interesting options for any areas requiring a temporary facility.

SERVERS, OPERATING SYSTEMS, AND DATABASES

As computers have proliferated, become less expensive, and applications have become more diverse, software designs have segregated computational activities. Some computers interact with users; others manage the storage of data, collect data from instruments, or assist in the organization of information. *Servers* are a class of computers with large computational and storage capacities that manage, store, and retrieve data for other computers. These include managing databases that service other computers. *Clients* are computers which interact directly with users, processing information to/from the server and sending/collecting information from users. The combination of these two types of computers constitutes a design called a *client–server* system. Because of their larger capacities and greater environmental needs, servers often reside in a data center. A client may act as an agent that collects and integrates data from several different servers.

An *operating system* is software designed to provide basic services to interface the hardware with applications software. Modern operating systems also provide user interfaces for graphics, the mouse, data networks, e-mail, and browser software. Common operating systems include Microsoft Windows, Apple OS X, and Linux. Clients and servers may use the same operating system software, differing mainly in two aspects. First, the computational capability and the storage capacity of the server are usually larger and second, different applications software run on servers and clients.

Real-time computers and operating systems are those designed to collect, manage, and in some cases, analyze and store data from "the real world" in a timely manner. Examples include data from EKG instruments, intravenous pumps, or monitors controlling the operation of an automobile engine. If data from these devices are missed, the device malfunctions. Real-time computers may interface to servers which are not real-time. For example, EKG data collected from monitors can be sent to an electronic medical record system.

Clients, real-time computers, and servers typically interchange data through a *data network*. The data network is a high-speed connection between two or more computers, usually through a copper or fiber-optic cable through which data are exchanged. A public network is one where access to or from computers outside the organization is relatively unrestricted. A private network is one where access is much more restricted. The Internet is probably the best known public network. Public networks may require additional security precautions since the unrestricted access to computers permit malicious activities. For example, real-time systems over a public network are vulnerable to service disruptions, so such an approach requires meticulous design, and is not optimal for a critical life-support system.

Servers require constant attention and periodic maintenance. Daily activities required for a large server farm include reviewing log files for problems and errors and performing disk backups, all of which can consume large amounts of time. Disk backups, where the contents of disks are copied to tape or another disk, protect against accidental loss of data. Backup disks are used to restore data should the original disks fail or data is otherwise destroyed. Periodic maintenance includes vendor updates or patches, mostly to correct or address problems or to introduce new features. These patches must be tested and applied. Vendors also release major new versions of operating systems and databases every 2–4 years. To receive vendor support for operating systems and databases, users must use the current versions of the software. Updating software consumes significant resource any organization. Finally, hardware requires replacement every 4–5 years, initiating an additional sequence of activities. It is not unusual for organization to spend 50–80% of their time on these maintenance activities.

Major hardware and software upgrades are particularly disruptive and challenging. Usually, new hardware must be installed while the old hardware continues to be used. The data center, in effect, must have the capacity to run both the new and old systems concurrently. Applications and system software (i.e., the operating system and database) must be installed and tested. Finally, the database must be migrated and converted from the old to the new system. In addition to the work building and testing the new system, the conversion of large databases requires long periods of downtime. Reducing the downtime to hours (e.g., under a single day) requires creativity. It is common for users to simply leave data on an old computer system, using both concurrently rather than migrating data. As computer databases become more complex and increase to hundreds of terabytes in size, migration will inevitably become more difficult.

MANAGING THE DESKTOP CLIENT

Desktop clients are desktop computers (or personal computers) configured to run one or more specialized clinical, business, and/or office applications. Client applications typically communicate with a server through a network and service a single user at a time. Clients may be shared by several users or may be dedicated to a single user.

Thin-clients are stripped down desktop clients designed so that they can be installed and managed as a simplified user managed appliance. Thin-clients may lack a local disk, load start-up software from hardware memory called firmware, and depend on the network and a central server to load other software. A web thin-client for example, only runs a web browser and depends on the web server for downloading small programs, such as applets, or any other application. The simplicity of thin-clients reduces desktop support requirements and eliminates most software configuration and updating, but in other ways they are managed similar to full-function desktops. Some applications, however, require redesign to function properly and others may not function properly at all, thus reducing their benefit.

CONFIGURATION STANDARDIZATION

Because of the large number of client computers in the typical hospital and their need for frequent attention, managing clients is challenging. For example, an average hospital and clinic supporting an extensive portfolio of third generation clinical and business applications will require nearly one personal computer for every employee using a computer. Most personal computers will require monthly updates to correct software defects and to protect against network attacks. A large hospital managing updates for 4000 desktop clients monthly will require a large number of support personnel if such updates are loaded one by one. Many applications also require that software be loaded and updated periodically, especially for their annual updates. Without an automated process, organizations are likely to perform this critical task infrequently, putting the organization at risk for vendor support or adverse events.

The benefits of standardized clients are significant. First, it is possible to test changes to the client and eliminate problems prior to their deployment. Problems can be debugged more predictably, assisting the help desk in both answering questions and fixing problems. The help desk staff can be more responsive and efficient. Replacement of defective devices has also been simplified by reducing the number of required replacement systems.

Standardization is the first step to ease management of client computers. Standardization refers to the development of a single software configuration for the desktop. This may include a fixed configuration of the operating system, applications software, and the minimum hardware needed. Depending on the software design of the desktop client, the configuration should be tolerant of changes in hardware which are already installed or likely to be installed. Hardware vendors introduce new designs every 6 months, and many administrators equate standardized hardware with a standardized configuration. Standardizing hardware on a particular vendor and model is difficult, expensive, and does not necessarily promote the efficiencies desired for a standardized client. Standardizing on a hardware configuration, an operating system and its version (e.g., Intel Pentium with more than 2.8 gigahertz CPU and more than 2 gigabytes memory, Windows XP, service pack 2) is easier.

To develop a standardized client requires identification of required applications and a list of desired goals for the client. Often these goals include supportability of the desktop client, costs, and system security. For clinical users moving from computer to computer, all clients should ideally operate identically. Two or more standardized configuration (or images) may be required to satisfy most user needs, and a small number of users will require a custom configuration. UW Medicine has developed two standard client images, one to support users in a shared clinical environment such as a nursing station, and a second supporting the office environment. The shared user image does not require users to login to the Windows client, depends on individual applications to provide authorization and authentication, and lacks common office applications such as word processing, presentation, and spreadsheet software. The office image allows users to perform all previous activities, requires a Windows logon, and supports typical office applications. These two configurations cover approximately half of the 10 000 supported clients. A standard desktop client will often support more applications than required by any single user. The disadvantages of having unused applications include increased software licensing costs, maintenance, and support complexity. Therefore, increased licensing costs may need to be balanced with higher levels of standardization. Frequently, users resist the migration to standardized systems since there is a perceived loss of flexibility. Designing clients through prototyping and obtaining user feedback minimizes this problem.

PATCHING, UPDATING, CLONING, AND INVENTORY

The large number of desktops requires that an organization perform routine activities with great efficiency. These activities include the building, updating, and managing the desktop. Building an initial desktop image from scratch can take several hours. Once this image has been built, it can be mass copied. Hardware disk copiers allow for high volume copying of this image in minutes. Disk copying software, such as Symantec's Ghost, allow for the deployment of a built image in 10–15 minutes. If the institution does not have the equipment or skills to build and deploy such a standard client, some vendors will provide this service. For example, large PC distributors can take a user image and deliver equipment tested and ready to deploy for a minimal additional charge (e.g., $25 per workstation).

Most organizations will also install central management software to manage, update, and monitor the desktop clients. A product, such as Microsoft's System Management Server (SMS), allows a central console to monitor and inventory clients and their installed software, apply patches, and provide other management functions. Typically, clients are required to have installed and to run a special software "stub" to permit the central server to perform its management functions. An inventory is particularly important because it can be used to locate misconfigured or defective systems.

There have been several interesting consequences to use of centrally managed desktops in our institution. First, users frequently move computers from their original locations, making routine maintenance more difficult, if not impossible. A second side effect has been the ability to routinely update the screen saver so as to provide messages to users. Third, the management software has helped identify hardware and software still being used and in some cases should be replaced, helping the capital planning process. This also has value in troubleshooting problems by identifying vulnerable configurations.

LIFE CYCLE AND DESKTOP REPLACEMENT ISSUES

The large number of desktop clients in most institutions requires a systematic approach for managing replacement. If the desktop computers have a predicted life of 4 years (generous for a desktop computer) and has 4000 desktop computers, then 1000 desktops must be replaced annually. If each costs $1000, the institution must budget $1 000 000 every year to keep up with desktop replacements, and this cost does not include the labor for identifying and replacing the systems. Continuous replacement of desktops is easier for personnel to manage and resource, but results in greater hardware heterogeneity; a "big-bang" replacement insures more hardware homogeneity, but is more difficult to resource. Some institutions have no formal replacement process and wait until the computers break or are not longer useful. Outdated hardware and operating systems create a support nightmare and can put critical patient-care activities at risk.

WINDOWS, LINUX, AND MACINTOSH CLIENTS

In spite of its deficiencies, many applications software in the health-care industry use Microsoft's Windows operating system, mainly because tools are available for controlling, managing, and cloning a large base of desktops. The Apple Macintosh platform is very popular among the research and academic community, and the public domain "freeware" Linux is used for many specialized applications, such as instruments. Cloning and central support may be more difficult to apply across a heterogeneous base of Macintosh and Linux clients, and hardware and operating system changes for the Macintosh may not be backward compatible. Unfortunately, the Windows platform suffers greater vulnerability from network attacks and requires greater vigilance on the part of those supporting it.

LAPTOPS

For workflow in which clinicians roam, such as patient rounding or the management of movable devices such as intravenous pumps, laptops and other portable devices can be invaluable. Unfortunately, laptops carry significant liabilities. First, they are more difficult to manage since they can be carried away. Maintenance, such as patching, updating, and inventory, are also more difficult, especially since many assumptions made for maintenance do not apply. Laptops, most importantly, should be designed and used so that if they are stolen, they do not hold patient or other private information.

Second, laptops cost about twice that of a desktop and have a lifespan of only 2–3 years, or about half as long as a desktop. When a keyboard or monitor breaks in a desktop, it can be replaced, but a similar repair in a laptop requires a trip back to the factory or a service call. Laptop batteries frequently require annual replacement at a cost of $100–200 each. Lastly, users drop laptops with predictable outcomes.

Third, the laptop has security vulnerabilities secondary to its portability. Many recent public security compromises in health-care organizations, including the VA, have been associated with laptops stolen from automobiles or briefcases with private information. Shared laptops, such as those being used for practitioner order entry during rounding, are more vulnerable to theft since there is no responsible owner. The usual techniques of physically securing a computer will make a laptop inconvenient or impossible to use as a portable device. Document encryption, where access to a document requires a password or passphrase, slows down file access, inconveniences document interchange, and becomes disastrous should the user forgets the password or passphrase. Although it is unclear that such devices significantly improve security, manufacturers even offer a biometric identification device such as a fingerprint reader.

SECURITY

Information security implements protection of valuable information system assets against abuse and improper use. There is a wide array of technological solutions that address security, and the solutions can indeed be very expensive; therefore, an approach that measures risks to the assets and implements cost effective controls to address the more significant risks is a practical approach. The risk-based approach requires the following: Understand critical *assets*, identify realistic *threats* to such assets, implement and enhance *controls* that protect assets against threats in presence of *vulnerabilities*, measure and mitigate residual *risks*, and handle *incidents* when threats are realized. These concepts and relationships are shown in the following figure, and are investigated in detail shortly.

Conceptually, security comprises of confidentiality, integrity, and availability of information assets. *Confidentiality* of a system requires

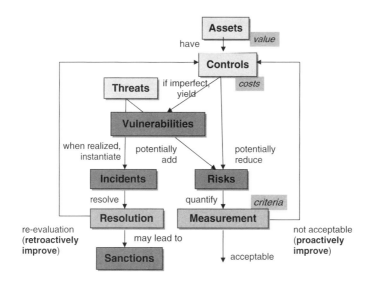

that information is accessed by authorized users of the information, and no unauthorized user is permitted to access information. Commonly implemented User ID and Password (a component of authentication) is a control to implement confidentiality. *Integrity* requires that information is not manipulated or changed in an unauthorized way. A systematic way of introducing changes to information system programs and configuration (also known as Change Control) is a control to implement integrity. *Availability* requires that information is available as and where it is necessary. Backup and recovery are common technical controls to protect against unexpected loss of data and therefore to implement availability. This section focuses on confidentiality; integrity and availability concepts are discussed variously in "Managing the desktop client," "Backup, redundancy, disaster planning, and recovery," and "Operations."

Information security is a dynamic operational activity in the Internet age, where technology changes every quarter, and new vulnerabilities and threats are identified daily. For example, wireless technology is quietly changing how care is provided at the bed side or at home, how providers access clinical information, or how assets are tracked using radio frequency identification (RFID) methods, but security aspects of the technology is only partially understood because threat models are still evolving. Another related example is legal requirement of "eDiscovery:" creation of a compendium of all electronic communication and data generated or received by an official which are then used in arguments for a legal case. Thus security professionals must continuously learn about new technologies and legislative progress to recognize and address changes in the information systems landscape.

Risk-based approach to security permits organizations to determine their risk tolerance limits while addressing all assets and threats in a comprehensive manner. The discipline of an organization determines whether risks are measured and addressed for all assets, whether required controls are uniformly implemented for all assets, and whether the risk evaluation is repeated often to stay current with technological changes. These functions comprise the operational aspect of implementing and monitoring security through controls.

ASSETS

Information assets are data, hardware and software systems that store, manipulate and transfer data, and physical enclosures and areas that hold these systems. Clinical data and images of patients, a payroll system, a web server that holds institutional web presence for its customers, desktop workstations, wireless access points, data centers that house institutional servers, and data closets that house network switches and routers are all examples of information assets. Assets often exist in hierarchical relationships: data are stored within a database; a database is part of an application; an application is a collection of programs running on a set of computers; and computers are part of a network.

Assets have value for the organization because they contribute towards financial and operational functions of the organization. Clearly, not all assets are of equal value; the value depends upon the context in which an asset is used, and whether there is redundancy, and other alternate methods to accomplish the same tasks. For example, the web server that holds the institutional web presence is less important than the payroll system, unless the institutional business is entirely dependent on the web presence (for example, Amazon). Similarly, all clinical data are important, but in general hospital context, laboratory data followed by radiology and pharmacy data may be considered as more important than others. But in Intensive Care Unit or in the Operating Rooms, the physiologic monitoring systems may be the most important.

In terms of security, the data and systems with higher value should be considered for better controls to protect confidentiality, integrity, and availability. For clinical systems, during a disaster, the value may determine the order in which systems are restored, implying lower availability for systems that are less important.

THREATS

A threat to an asset is any action, active or passive, that alters or denies the proper behavior or function of the asset. Threats may be classified along different criteria. A threat may be malicious, or accidental, or opportunistic in nature depending upon the intent of harm. A threat may be carried out by an internal or an external user or agent. A threat may have incidental, significant, or debilitating impact depending upon its harm potential.

Here are some real examples of threats.

  Someone from the Internet exploits an internal server to distribute copyrighted media illegally to other Internet users. Here the perpetrator may be opportunistic in taking advantage of an available server, is an external agent, and the threat may be significant in its use of the storage media resources.

  Some internal user is abusing their privilege to look up personal identification information (such as social security number and address) of wealthy patients to conduct credit fraud. This is a malicious activity by an internal user with significant impact.

  Someone drops coffee on their desktop which is regularly backed up. This is an accidental activity by an internal user with incidental impact.

  A construction worker trips over a power cable in the data center pulling the cable out. This is an accidental activity by an external agent with debilitating impact.

Common network and systems-related threats are infrastructural threats from the Internet which are well understood in the information security world. Significant among them are virus and spyware programs, which have evolved into "Bot" threats. Bots infect local computers which are remotely controlled (maliciously or opportunistically) by an external agent from distant and even foreign master controller computers, and these slave or "zombie" computers are anonymously used to send spam, or conduct distributed attacks on other computers.

In healthcare, one domain-specific threat to patient records is driven by human curiosity towards information about celebrities or about families and acquaintances. The information thus obtained without a "need to know" may then be used for malicious purposes. A second threat is identity theft because confidential information such as social security number is prevalent (and sometimes necessary for billing) in health-care data collections.

CONTROLS AND VULNERABILITY

Controls are placed on assets to protect them against a variety of threats. Controls are specific to assets and their use. Controls can be technological such as user sign on (authentication), or procedural such as change control procedure, or based on personnel training such as teaching "safe use of Internet" to the workforce. Controls may have automated or manual steps; technological controls are typically automated, procedural and technology-based controls may have both automated and manual components. Controls are not perfect—there may be unknown threats; there may be limitations because of the way assets are constructed (such as software bugs) or used (such as configuration weakness); and they may be extremely expensive.

Vulnerabilities in a control are specific ways to access or abuse the asset by working around the controls and exploiting their imperfections. A threat may exploit one or several vulnerabilities to attack an asset. As mentioned before, assets often exist in a hierarchy. A vulnerability in a control for an asset may be mitigated fully or partially by another control on a higher level asset. The concept of multiple controls at multiple levels (network level, computer level, application level, and data level) is known as *defense in-depth,* which is necessary for effective security.

Manufacturers of well-known operating systems such as Windows and MacOS, and databases such as Oracle and Microsoft SQL publish their vulnerabilities periodically, and issue patches and upgrades to address them.

Here are some examples of technological controls.

Network level controls

Network firewalls implement limited connectivity between internal network and the Internet and networks of other partner organizations, permitting only the necessary communication and protecting against network probing and reconnaissance by external agents.

Network Intrusion Detection and Prevention Systems (IDPS) passively monitor network traffic, detect malicious activities, and if detected, create alerts and take active steps to eliminate the threat by either denying the malicious traffic, or logically removing the malicious computer from the network. IDPS can be *signature-based* where a network communication contents match a known pattern or signature of a known threat or attack.

A threat sometimes exploits a vulnerability that is yet to be identified or corrected by the manufacture and a signature may not exist as yet. Such a threat is called a *zero-day threat* (or *attack*). IDPS can also be *behavior-based* where network communication patterns are monitored against their usual, normal behavior. An aberration in behavior pattern may indicate a malicious activity, typically exhibited by zero-day attacks.

Network access authentication implements a sign on before a computer is permitted to logically join the internal network. It is more commonly used for wireless networks.

Virtual private networks implement an authenticated, encrypted, and limited communication from an external untrusted computer or network to internal network, and are often used to connect from home and remote computers.

Network access control implements network access authentication as well as a dynamic vulnerability scanning and detection when a computer joins a network, and if the joining computer is found to be vulnerable, then the computer is placed in a separate, quarantine network permitting only the remediation of the vulnerabilities such as downloading patches, implement anti-virus software, etc.

Computer level controls

Authentication implements a user sign on before a user is permitted to use any resource on the computer. The authentication typically requires a matched *user ID* and *password*, and optionally a physical token such as a smart card which makes authentication stronger. The password should never be stored in clear text in any system. Often in organizational networks, the authentication on a desktop is managed by a network server (such as Microsoft Active Directory server) which consolidates the user IDs and passwords, and such an authentication is commonly referred to as *network sign on*.

Authorization implements rules about a user's ability to access specific resources within the computer. For example, a user is permitted to read certain files but not update them. Authorization is specific to the user, and therefore requires authentication for correct identification.

Audit logs implement a log of what activities were actually conducted by a user for a retrospective view. In case a real security breach occurs, audit logs provide the ability to conduct *postmortem* for the breach. *Security event/incident management (SEIM)* systems permit logs from diverse systems (network devices such as routers, firewalls, switches, and wireless controllers; operating systems such as Unix, Windows, and Mainframe/MVS; directories such as Active Directory and SunOne Java Directory Server; databases such Oracle and Microsoft SQL) to be collected real time to one central server to conduct automated monitoring and reporting.

Patching is the process of updating software when the manufacturer issues a patch for a vulnerability. In a network, central patch servers are deployed to update hundreds of desktops simultaneously. It is important to first test application software with patches separately for compatibility before releasing the patch. Also, the patches should be applied reasonably quickly after they are released. An up-to-date computer is a good protection against viruses and spyware.

Host-based firewalls and intrusion detection and prevention system, similar to their Network counterparts, limit network communication for one computer (the host) and attempt to detect and prevent malicious activities within the computer. One important class of such software is anti-virus software which detect and prevent virus and spyware.

Encryption technologies like secure sockets layer (SSL), secure shell (SSH), etc. are used to encrypt data in transmission between computers. *Encryption and hashing algorithms* may be used to encrypt and digitally sign files and data at rest.

Application and data level controls

Authentication, authorization, and *audit logs* are applicable controls at the application level. Considering the large number of applications in healthcare, multiple sign ons can become a significant burden to the users. Commercial *single sign on* technologies solve multiple sign on problems but they can be expensive. In healthcare, the Clinical Context Object Work-group (CCOW) standard under ANSI HL7 addresses multiple sign on for health-care applications. If an application is CCOW compliant, appropriate user context (and patient context) within one application is automatically transferred to a second application when it is started; no authentication (and patient selection) in the second application is necessary. With the advent of Regional Health Information Organizations (RHIO), where patient data may be accessed across autonomous organizations, a *federated model* of authentication will be necessary where one organization will trust authentication at another organization within a limited context.

In health-care applications, the operating principles of clinical data access are "need to know" and "minimum necessary." In large health-care organizations, it is impractical to precisely determine authorization relationships *a priori* that match thousands of users and thousands of patients, *and* to keep them up to date while clinical care requirements change. In fact, a strict and limited authorization scheme will adversely impact clinical care. Therefore, authorization rules in healthcare are necessarily more permissive.

Accordingly, audit logs are even more important in health-care context. Similar to IDPS, the application level logs may be analyzed for anomalous behavior to detect inappropriate access. Examples of items to monitor will include access to celebrity patients and employees. Again, because there are a large number of health-care applications, audit logs from all applications should first be collected together in an application level SEIM system for monitoring and reporting.

RISK ASSESSMENT

Risk assessment is a systematic procedure to assess whether there are sufficient controls placed on assets that meet the organization's risk tolerance criteria. It is an accounting of whether the controls are effective, and whether sufficient consideration and deliberation has been made towards deficiencies to make an informed decision about residual risks. There are no universally acceptable criteria for risk measures; each industry evolves towards a spectrum of best practices based upon their collective experiences with threats, assets, costs, and benefits. An academic medical center is different from a community hospital which is different from a physician's office. Accordingly, the assets, controls, resources, and organizational risk perspectives are significantly different in these different settings.

Each organization must formalize its security expectations into a set of information security policies and procedures. Especially for new technologies or business processes, creation of a policy is an organizationally collective and informed decision taking into account how the organization's peers are addressing the same issue. These policy and procedures specify parameters for the controls, and consequences if controls are not in place or inadequate.

Risk evaluation methods assess the completeness of institutional policies, and construct a risk questionnaire based on the contents of policies and procedures. Questionnaires may be specific to asset classes, and may be addressed for each asset, such as important applications, or for an asset class where assets are configured similarly, such as desktops or networking switches and routers. The evaluation can be conducted in different ways: (1) self-evaluation where the asset administrators report on asset configuration and operation; (2) evaluation by an internal organizational group (information security, risk management, internal audit, etc.); and (3) evaluation by an external group (external auditors, security consultants, etc.).

Evaluation should consider both direct answers as well as answers of related questions on related assets to identify a full picture of control efficacy, and a true estimate of the risk. Due to *defense in-depth* principle, one risk may be addressed significantly by another control on a related asset. In some evaluation methods, questions are labeled on importance: *high*, *medium*, or *low*. Sometimes, the answers may satisfy the intent of the question: *fully*, *partially*, or *'does not.'* By assigning numeric scores to these criteria, each asset can be assigned an aggregate score by adding scores of all questions, which provides a simple way to represent risk. By considering scores of similar assets in a spectrum, an organization can determine its risk acceptance criteria for an asset class.

Once risks are assessed and measured, there are three ways to address them. *Risk acceptance* is a formal step of accepting the residual risks with understanding and in agreement of administrators and owners of the asset. *Risk mitigation* is enhancing controls for the assets as well as identifying and implementing compensating controls to related assets to reduce risks. *Risk transference* is acquiring insurance against possible monetary losses due to information security problems.

SECURITY INCIDENTS AND SANCTIONS

An *information security incident* occurs when a threat becomes real and an asset is compromised. An incident is also known as a *security breech*. Incidents may be identified through automated monitoring systems such as IDPS or SEIM, or may be manually detected such as non-availability of an asset. Security incidents are reported also by personnel as they observe practices in their workplace.

A *security incident procedure* is required to evaluate security incidents. The procedure defines types of incidents based on its impact and virulence. Impact may be measured in terms of number of computers involved, or number of users who are denied a resource, or a highly important asset. Virulence may be classified by extent of service disruption caused by the incident. Both have to be determined in real-time as incident is identified.

It is necessary to first isolate the attack to reduce its malicious activities to protect the rest of the assets. Subsequently, a *root cause analysis* is conducted to pinpoint the actual control failure or deficiency that caused the attack to succeed, and to improve the controls to prevent a future incident.

An incident may also be caused by an individual accidentally or maliciously. It is necessary that a *sanctions policy* be in place that provides adequate steps to reeducate, warn, and if necessary, terminate employment of the individual. It is important that the policy is equally applied to all employees. In some cases such as identity fraud, law enforcement agencies should be involved for any possible legal action.

There are many federal regulations governing clinical computing system security in a medical center. Some include

- Health Insurance Reform: Security Standards; Final Rule (also known as HIPAA, part 3) [2];
- FDA 21 CFR Part 11. Guidance for Industry, Part 11, Electronic Records; Electronic Signatures—Scope and Application [3] and
- Sarbanes–Oxley Act of 2002 [4];
- IRB/Common Rule [5].

Finally, many standards organizations and professional societies have developed guidelines promoting good practices in managing information systems. Many IT audit organizations use these standards. These include

- International Organization for Standardization (ISO) ISO/IEC 17799 and ISO/DIS 27799 Health informatics [6]
- National Institute of Standards and Technology (NIST) [7] and
- COSO/CobiT audit standards.

BACKUP, REDUNDANCY, DISASTER PLANNING,
AND RECOVERY

RELIABILITY, AVAILABILITY, AND REDUNDANCY

Reliability is the measure of a computer system, or one or more of its components, to be free from failure. One measurement of a computer system's reliability is *downtime*, the percentage or amount of time that a computer system is down, or *uptime*, the percentage or time that a computer system has been up. With complex computer systems and networks, it may be difficult to define and measure reliability, uptime, or downtime. *Availability* measures the amount that a system is functionally usable and may be more relevant to users since a system may be operational, but unavailable. Reliability numbers should always be higher than availability. Examples of situations when a system is operational, but unavailable include times associated with software maintenance.

To improve reliability computer systems or their components can be replicated. Redundancy increases the number of components, and can result in increased component level failures, but properly designed, system failures decrease. For example, redundant array of inexpensive disks (RAID) is a disk drive technology which uses redundancy to improve reliability [8]. One configuration uses three disks to handle the capacity of two. The three drives will have failures a third more often than a system with two drives, but because of the low probability that two drives will fail simultaneously, system failure is reduced.

A system with 99% reliability operating 24 hours/day 7 days/week will have 87.6 hours of annual downtime. 99.9% reliability equals 8.76 hours of annual downtime. Unexpected downtime is less acceptable than scheduled downtime during low periods of patient activity. A critical patient care system with 99% availability and going down 1.7 hours each week in an unscheduled manner is unacceptable, even if this occurs each night when patient activity is low since finding a low activity time may be impossible. Most hardware today will operate with very high levels of reliability; unfortunately, software failures, human failures, and routine maintenance activities can adversely impact computer system availability.

AVAILABILITY, FAILURES, AND BACKUPS

With increasing complex computer systems, availability and its measurement has become increasingly complex. Availability can be viewed as three layers, all of which are dependent on lower layers for its operation. At the lowest level, the computer hardware and its environment, including data networks, impacts availability. Layered above the hardware are operating systems and closely associated software such as databases. At the highest level is the applications software interfacing with the user. Since the applications software layer is the most complex, most system failures are likely to occur there rather than at the hardware or environmental level. Errors associated with human factors particularly permeate the development and use of application software including those associated with software development, debugging, implementation, user training, and errors in its use [9].

Data center failures have been discussed previously and are uncommon, even for a tier 1 computer room. Hardware failures which shut systems down are equally rare. High failure components include electromechanical devices such as disk drives, tape drives, and cooling fans, and power supplies, which converts incoming AC power to low DC voltages. Most servers are equipped or can be equipped so that disk drives are monitored and replicated so that a single device failure does not result in a system failure. Tape drives can be designed so that they can be replaced while the system is operational. Likewise, most servers have redundant power supplies or can be equipped with redundant power supplies. If a particular server will be used in an application requiring high availability, the user should specify options which provide for redundancy and "hot-swapping," e.g., the ability to replace components while the system is use. By far, data network interruptions comprise the most common failures at the hardware level. Interruptions in the network may be physical, such as cutting of a wire, or logical, such as a failure induced by excessive network traffic (a "network storm" or a "denial of service attack" or DOS).

Operating systems and databases, like hardware, can and will fail. Failures in operating systems and databases are more complex, and are typically caused by software errors or defects causing the system to fail (crash) and possibly corrupt its data. Failures in operating systems and databases may not be resolved through redundancy, and using redundancy often requires substantial technical skills. Operating systems and databases can also be *mirrored or clustered,* two techniques where two or more systems run in parallel with each other, providing redundancy and/or increased capacity.

Unfortunately, redundancy in an operating system or database may result in the same failure in two systems unless one of the operating systems avoids the precipitating event(s). In a mirrored system, the same failure is likely to occur in both systems since they are processing events in parallel. To insure reliability, the duplicated database should be delayed, lagging behind the primary database by hours, so that the precipitating event can be avoided. The disadvantage of this approach, of course, is that if the primary system fails, the secondary system must catch-up before it is ready.

To insure that recovery from database errors can occur, databases, in conjunction with the underlying operating system, can perform functions designed to preserve and recover data. These include periodic *checkpointing*, where critical data needed for recovery are periodically saved. Checkpointing can occur every few minutes, thus protecting systems from a significant data loss, but this exacts an undesirable performance overhead. A list of activities performed on the database will usually be stored in log files. Log files may be *rolled forward*, to catch a system up to the current time, or it may be *rolled backward*, so as to backup the database to the pre-error condition.

Certain failures, however, may prevent these functions from performing their activities properly. One avenue for protection is a redundant system running a delayed backup database. A more traditional avenue is a *backup*, a copy of the operational disk drives transferred to a second set of disk drives or to magnetic tape media. With tape media, multiple backups can be created, allowing data to be retained for years and significant capability to recover from disastrous errors. Unfortunately, restoration of disk images from tape (or even anther set of disks) can be very time consuming, and are being performed so infrequently that backup restoration becomes a lost art. With RAIDs, checkpoints, and other safeguards, it is not unusual that tape restores have not been performed for more than a decade.

Checkpoints and other database tools can be very effective in protecting against failures caused by applications software. Likewise, hardware redundancy usually protects systems from hardware failures. Many applications software requires frequent updates, and these updates often require downtimes. Often, the redundant system provides access to older data during times when the primary system is being updated, rather than provide backups for a failed system. For example, a backup system can provide access to older patient data in an EMR software update requiring 6 hours of downtime.

DISASTERS, DISASTER RECOVERY, AND BUSINESS CONTINUITY

The importance of clinical computing systems in patient care has raised the awareness of their vulnerabilities and the need of these systems to be operational during a disaster. A robust computer environment depends on the ability of both the IT and clinical teams to:

1. Anticipate areas of vulnerability;
2. Understand the vulnerabilities and impacts on the organization;
3. Identify required services;
4. Set priorities for required services; and
5. Take actions to ameliorate vulnerabilities subject to priorities and cost effectiveness.

Robustness requires that appropriate planning, training, and actions be taken by both the IT and clinical teams. Although the technology to build a computer facility which can withstand any disaster may be possible, it is usually not realistic or cost effective to build it.

Disaster recovery refers to those contingency plans for recovering computer systems following a major disaster such as a hurricane, earthquake, or fire, or any other cause resulting in the prolonged loss of a computer system. Options include

1. *Revert to manual processes.* Although this may require the least initial investment by an organization, it may be only be partially effective in recovering critical data stored in failed system(s), and the ability to restore an organization to full functionality may be impossible.
2. *Maintain a hot backup site.* In this option, a system in a remote location operates in a standby mode until it is needed. Hot backups are expensive since equipment remains largely unused except in an emergency. Damage to required infrastructure, such as that caused by earthquakes, can may result in the hot backup site being inaccessible even if it is operational, since communications links are often lost following a major disaster.
3. *Selectively maintain critical systems in a redundant fashion.* Clinical data varies in their importance. In this approach, the user identifies critical information and designs systems so that the most valuable data is readily available. Prioritize tasks to make the most important information available first.

Disaster recovery plans must address both short-term and longer-term needs for the restoration of the organization. For example, the short-term needs for a hospital might be to restart the EMR and telephone equipment to provide patient care for the injured and to communicate with emergency transportation services. A slightly longer-term requirement will be the issuing of paychecks and the restoration of purchasing functions to acquire supplies and services.

Business continuity refers to those activities required to continue the functioning of the institution. These may include both IT and non-IT activities, and typically address the needs of an organization on a longer timeframe. Of particular importance is the recognition that there are no simple formulas for disaster planning and business continuity. Expensive business continuity solutions may be highly ineffective if personnel are poorly trained in its execution. Likewise, simple manual procedures may be highly effective, especially in situations where immediate patient care and trauma are the primary considerations.

In spite of the complexity of any disaster recovery and business continuity plan, certain basic information contributes to success. A good inventory of computers, including clients, servers, and applications allows for identification of servers and the software they service. Systems must be prioritized (i.e., clients can be categorized into critical patient care and administrative). In critical situations, working clients can be moved to support critical applications, regardless of their original use. Most important, everyone must understand priorities and be skilled in performing needed actions.

With regards to disaster recovery and business continuity, we have chosen to classify servers into one of five categories:

1. Critical system such that a downtime of several hours will seriously impact patient care;
2. Important secondary system supporting patient care or critical administrative system;
3. System is operationally important, but some unavailability can be tolerated;
4. Training or some other system which can tolerate significant unavailability; and
5. Test or any other system which can be left off without consequences.

In a disaster situation, this information will help identify:

1. Critical systems to restart after a massive outage. Restarting complex systems can take time with skilled personnel. It is important to use such resources appropriately.
2. Non-critical systems to shutdown to conserve cooling and power. UPS batteries, backup generators, and chillers may not

have full capacity in an emergency. Reduced loads allow them to operate longer.

3. Critical systems and the information to mirror. It may be more cost effective to provide special subsystems which only provide a critical subset of patient care information rather than the full electronic medical record.

In more elaborate designs, servers and computer facilities can reconfigure themselves to recover from and in response to disasters either automatically or in response to a central command. For example, a computer room can be configured to pull in backup cooling units in the event of high temperature. If this fails, unneeded servers are shut down in a predetermined fashion.

The most important aspect in any disaster, however, lies in the ability of an organization and its staff to operate in the absence of one or more computer-based services. Organizations transition from manual to automated systems over decades. One consequence of a successful transition, unfortunately, is the lost of knowledge and skills associated with manual workflows and procedures. Ironically, a flawed computer design resulting in moderate periods of unavailability can facilitate disaster responsiveness through forcing an organization to understand, develop, and practice such procedures.

OPERATIONS

As with most aspects of information technology, people perform critical tasks to support and maintain the infrastructure. These activities range from routine day-to-day tasks, to infrequent highly skilled troubleshooting, and finally those to anticipate, plan, budget, optimize, and replace/refresh resources at the organizational level. Some have high visibility, such as those associated with a help desk answering the telephone. Neglecting other less visible activities, such as the planning for data centers or replacement of older systems, may become apparent only after years, or in some cases, decades. Organizations often fail to recognize the attention that information technology requires, and that the total costs of a maintaining a system over its life will exceed its initial purchase price. For the purposes of this section, the staffing of the organization will be segmented into: (1) daily operations, including the help desk, support of desktop systems, and data center operations; (2) periodic operations, including software and hardware maintenance including server maintenance and upgrades, infrastructure systems, and emergency and trouble shooting procedures; and (3) organizational operations, including project planning and anticipating needs on a longer time frame.

High costs and difficulty in skills needed to maintain an IT organization have resulted in some hospitals subcontracting the help desk and other operations to vendors or third party contractors. Such contracts can result in short-term budgetary savings, but the impacts in the longer term, such as on the retention of key organizational skills, are unclear. Contractors may defer major costs without impacts becoming apparent until much later. For example, Dell Corporation moved their call centers overseas to reduce costs. Dell pulled back many of these call centers in 2003 when service complaints increased. In the meantime, Dell lost business because of poor service [10].

DAILY OPERATIONS

Information technology organizations require that staff handle a number of daily routine activities. For users, this includes the troubleshooting, management, and possibly the replacement of the desktop client. At the front line is the *help desk or call center*, which typically receives the initial telephone or e-mail request. This is the public face of an IT organization and provides a critical service to insure the success of clinical information systems. Unfortunately, it frequently receives less attention than it deserves.

Most users calling a help desk have requests falling into one of three areas: (1) an expired password or other system access problems; (2) trouble using an application; or (3) equipment problems. Ideally, the person answering the call can handle most or all user problems. In a larger organization, these tasks may require different skills or people located in other parts of an organization. Compounding this, personnel staffing call centers are often "entry level," often trained on the job and with relatively high turnover. This results in limiting call center responsibilities to simple tasks and "call forwarding" most others. Multiple wait queues frustrate users, and these steps add delays to handling a relatively simple problem. On the other hand, using higher skilled personnel increases expenses, and these staff dislike the routine nature of a call center. Call centers are often located remote from clinical areas and are dependent on others for assessment of problems.

Reducing help desk calls requires analysis and planning, and usually time to correct the problems. Call statistics should be analyzed for possible resolutions. For example, the cause of frequent desktop failures should be analyzed and repaired. If the cause centers to a certain configuration or the age of a system, these problems can be targeted. A web site can allow users to recover lost or expired passwords and even create new accounts, greatly reducing help desk calls. Assistance with complex applications, such as the EMR, can be more difficult. Often help desk personnel are familiar with common office applications, but not complex clinical applications. Low cost options include tutorials on the use of a system, such as through a web site or through newsletters or e-mails. More expensive options include classroom tutorials. Probably the most effective and most expensive option is having designated "super users" on call to provide assistance to those having problems. If these are not dedicated resources, such calls may divert nurses or others from their principal responsibilities.

Supporting the desktop client (i.e., workstation) may fall into the responsibilities of the help desk or another desktop support group. In either case, the handoff should be transparent. If the desktop is robust and nursing units and outpatient clinics are designed to have extra systems, replacement of failed systems can be "next-day;" otherwise replacements may need to be within hours. Again staffing must balance costs and responsiveness, tradeoffs which most organizations find difficult. Most desktop failures are associated with mice, monitors, or keyboards. One option is to train clinical staff on their replacement and stock these relatively inexpensive components in a common supply area(s). Another role of the desktop group is the deployment of new or replacement systems. With a life cycle of 4–5 years, computer replacement will always be a large part of any mature organization. For example, University of Washington Medicine has more than 10 000 personal computers. This requires replacement of 2000 to 2500 systems annually or about ten systems daily. If the installation of a single PC requires 1 hour, this requires the resources of about two full-time staff. In most organizations, resource constraints limit support for systems purchased by a home user to only a few basic items. The hardware and software is likely to vary significantly from a standardized configuration, and the network environment is unknown. Therefore, areas which can be handled are those which are not associated with these factors such as resetting a password.

The help desk plays a key, but somewhat infrequent responsibility in the management of service outages. This includes routine downtimes, unexpected downtimes, and disasters. Therefore, the help desk should have a list of emergency telephone contacts, call schedules, and other tools designed to disseminate rapidly any needed notifications. These tools may include e-mail call lists and automatic pager systems. Unfortunately, personnel often become dependent on these tools, which in a major disaster, may be unavailable. Planning should recognize that services that depend on networks, such as e-mail and pager systems, can fail. Widespread deployment of telephones using Internet protocols (voice over Internet protocols or VOIP), due to their economic advantages, may make emergency operations particularly vulnerable to network or even power outages.

Data center operations include monitoring of computer rooms and their servers, networks, and security systems. Data centers be staffed or unstaffed ("lights out") or some combination of the both. Data center staff performs a number of activities. In addition to monitoring of the data center, staff may also be responsible for: (1) performing system backup, such as exchanging tapes; (2) wiring, installing, and removing systems; and (3) maintenance of computer facilities including cooling, power and fire detection, and suppression systems. During unstaffed times, data center monitoring may be performed by computer room environment monitors and specialized software monitoring servers. Depending on the complexity of their environment, data center and help desk operations may be performed by the same group or operate in such a manner as to provide cross-support for each other. The higher complexity of the data center requires that the staff be adequately trained. Most data center also requires a level of operational discipline and familiarity that staffing will take 3–6 months of local training in addition to skills in networking and server hardware.

INFRASTRUCTURE SUPPORT AND OTHER RELATED ACTIVITIES

Although not strictly operational in nature, certain infrastructure activities greatly improve the ability of the help desk and data center to operate. In addition to activities and software required to maintain clients and servers mentioned previously (e.g., patching), software for the help desk and data center operations, for example, are required for most organizations. Examples of these include software for: (1) the call center, (2) data center monitoring, (3) network monitoring, and (4) security logging and security monitoring. Substantial skill may be required to install and maintain these support systems. Automating these activities, however, greatly improves the reliability and consistency of infrastructure operations.

Call center software has become an integral part of most help desk operations. This software is designed to guide help desk personnel through the workflow of common tasks, and is available from both commercial and freeware sources. Standardized procedures for handling common calls are a prerequisite for the installation of these systems. Properly installed, these systems prioritize and communicate tasks to those performing the tasks and monitor their resource utilization and outcome. Sophisticated installations can even monitor user satisfaction. Unfortunately, a side effect of these systems is the focus on the number of outstanding calls, the number of open calls, and the speed in handling calls rather than the identification of the root cause of the problem and its mediation.

Software monitoring data center include those monitoring servers, networks, and security logs. Server monitors can report disk failures, warn of disks reaching capacity, excessive CPU utilization, and many other user-defined parameters. These monitors can then page support personnel and alert of problems. Defining parameters and the personnel to notify can be difficult, and often these systems fail because frequent alarms irritate staffs, who then turn off notifications. Network monitors can identify failed devices and virus compromised systems attacking other systems, allowing for the staff to replace or disable these systems to minimize their damage. Software can also download system logs and cross-examine them for evidence of attacks and compromise. Any successful "lights-out" operation requires substantial attention to automating monitoring activities.

ORGANIZATIONAL PLANNING AND OTHER HIGHER ORGANIZATIONAL OPERATIONS

Predicting, planning, and scheduling activities improve an organization's ability to be cost effective and responsive to the delivery of desired services. As an institution's compendium of information systems grow, the need to managing the resource increases. This need was recognized in the 1970s as systems expanded rapidly in banking and finance [11]. A large number of unscheduled projects greatly decrease coordination of activities and organizational cohesiveness as well as efficiency. Activities which can greatly enhance an organization's operational effectiveness include (1) short and long-term planning and budgeting for well-established operational activities; (2) change control and notifications to those impacted; and (3) intake and planning for new projects.

Predicting ongoing support costs is critical. For example, most computer hardware should be replaced in 5 years, and few last as long as 10 years. Therefore, budgets should include replacements for clients and servers based on a 5–10-year cycle. Associated operating systems are also likely to be impacted by these hardware replacements so this too should be budgeted. Network hardware also has a shorter 5-year replacement cycle, so it too needs to be considered in the operational baseline. Other costs include replacing UPS batteries every 2–4 years.

All software, likewise, requires routine maintenance and has associated costs. For many products, annual maintenance fees are levied by the vendor. Other products may require a periodic replacement or refresh. Under some support arrangements, for example, Microsoft does not charge an annual support fee, but the user is expected to upgrade software every 3–5 years by paying for a new license. Judging and budgeting personnel costs for maintenance should be included and can be more difficult. One industry consulting group has suggested that a single systems analyst can maintain 10–20 servers, but this ratio depends on the complexity of the tasks being performed [12]. Thus an organization with 600 servers could have a staff of more than 30 FTEs to just to do baseline maintenance on their servers. With servers costing under $10 000 each and salaries for skilled staff at $100 000/ year, the annual personnel costs for maintenance is $5000 or half of its purchase price! Likewise applications software, such as an EMR, requires maintenance. The metrics for this activity greatly depends on the application software and its implementation, but the costs are frequently even higher due to software complexity.

Change control requires that updates or changes to software, hardware, or other parts of the infrastructure or application go through testing and analysis of its expected and potential impacts. Those making the change are expected to test changes, understand impacts, notify users, and minimize unexpected side effects. Too often, ad hoc changes are made by individuals with little or no understanding of impacts. For example, an untested change in a source system can propagate through an interface and generate an error in a downstream EMR system.

Project intake and portfolio management are two closely related activities. Portfolio management is the process of maintaining a list of software used by an organization and other closely associated information. This information is instrumental to understanding the ongoing costs of maintaining systems, and the longer-term costs of replacing them. All systems have a life cycle, typically 10–20 years, and ultimately require replacement. The costs for replacement must be included in any long range view of an organization. Relevant information which should be included in a portfolio should include (1) name of the application, (2) purpose of application, (3) vendor, if any, (4) version number, (5) details of hardware running the application, such as their age, CPU, brand of server, operating system, location, etc., (6) network address(es), (7) date of last software update(s), and (8) any other information which helps in the operation and support of the system.

Project intake attempts to justify, cost, schedule, and resource new systems into an institution in an organized manner and to insure that these activities do not disrupt existing maintenance activities or other previously scheduled projects. Project intake should perform the following: (1) identify both the initial and ongoing *costs* for introducing a new system; (2) determine the *business case* for the project, including its return on investment; (3) assure that the system has received the support and *approvals* from appropriate management; (4) determine its potential *impact* on both IT and the organization; and in some cases (5) assign priorities for the project. Some of this information will be provided by IT, but most will be provided by a vendor or the user proposing the project. In most cases, project intake does not assess the value of the project. Prioritization and resources must be performed by other business units. Organizations with an effective project management process appear to require fewer resources for project planning since the management process has essentially identified and cleared resources needed for a new project, leaving only the details of coordinating resources.

Both project intake and portfolio management may be a simple informal or a highly structured processes. Informal approaches can work well in organizations with simple IT needs. Larger and more mature organizations with large portfolios, especially in governmental or large corporate environments, will require a more structured formalized process.

OUTSOURCING

Because of the complexity and costs of running and managing IT services, some hospitals have contracted or outsourced this work to vendors rather than staff and operate their own systems. Outsourcing services can range from defined activities such as an outside firm running a data center, operating the help desk, or supporting the data network to full service activities such as the contracting, installation, and operation of an EMR. Some software vendors will allow a user to implement their software on vendor-owned hardware so that the user can avoid the costs of buying hardware and running a data center. This option is often referred to as *remote hosting*. Outsourcing vendors include software companies, such as Epic or Cerner, and large IT service providers, such as EDS and IBM. Factors favoring outsourcing include (1) eliminates the hiring and management a technical staff; (2) vendors are more skilled with the software application(s) and are familiar with processes; (3) outsourcing can eliminate large cyclic capital outlays; and (4) more predictable and improved service levels. Arguments against outsourcing include (1) expense; (2) loss of skills and the ability to tailor applications to meet institutional needs; and (3) management of vendor is often problematic. The success of any organization on outsourcing depends on the service requested, the skills of the user to manage the vendor, and the skill of the vendor to perform the service. Massive outsourcing was popular several years ago, probably because several vendors offered highly favorable outsourcing contracts.

Outsourcing is likely to be cost effective for well circumscribed commodity services such as networking, but less effective for unusual or highly custom services, especially services for which the vendors are less unfamiliar. One study reported that 22% of 153 hospitals outsourced IT, only second to human resources. Areas outsourced included computer systems (31%), network management (25%), and help desk (13%) [13]. A problem reported with outsourcing was staff turnover, an ironic reason since the inability to hire staff is one major motivation to outsource.

SUMMARY

Infrastructure and security are critical components of any organization running an electronic medical record. These services provide the day-to-day operational support for the hardware and software. Properly supported, infrastructure competency allows an organization to maintain agility in responding to strategic directives and tactical changes.

The invisibility of many of infrastructure services may encourage an organization to ignore or defer tasks, and often the costs of catching-up can be significant. Although organizations can purchase services through outside contracted vendors, those developing skills in their own personnel can use resources more cost effectively, saving as much as 25–40% according to one Department of Defense study [14], particularly in areas such as disaster management. In the longer term, the use of contracted services can result in the loss of skills necessary for making strategic decisions, putting into question as to whether the estimated savings of contracting can be achieved [15].

REFERENCES

[1] Turner WP, Seader JH, and Brill KG. The Classifications Define Site Infrastructure Performance. Available at: http://www.upsite.com/TUIpages/whitepapers/tuitiers.html. accessed August 4, 2007.

[2] 45 CFR parts 160, 162, 164. Health Insurance Reform: Security Standards; Final Rule (also known as HIPAA, part 3). Department of Health and Human Services, Office of the Secretary. *Federal Register*. February 20, 2003; 68(34): 8334–80.

[3] 21 CFR part 11. Guidance for Industry, Part 11, Electronic Records; Electronic Signatures – Scope and Application. Department of Health and Human Services, Food and Drug Administration. August, 2003.

[4] H.R. 3863, Sarbanes–Oxley Act of 2002 (also known as the Public Company Accounting Reform and Investor Protection Act of 2002). 107th Congress, Second Session, January 23, 2002.

[5] 45 CFR 46. Title 45, Public Welfare, Department of Health and Human Services, National Institutes of Health, Office for Protection from Research Risks, Part 46, Protection of Human Subjects (also known as IRB Common Rule). *Federal Register*. November 13, 2001; 66(219): 56775–80.

[6] International Organization for Standardization (ISO) ISO/IEC 17799, ISO/DIS 27799 Health informatics – Information Security Management in Health Using ISO/IEC 17799. Available for purchase through http://www.iso.ch, accessed July 11, 2007.

[7] National Institute of Standards and Technology (NIST), Information Quality Standards. Available at http://www.nist.gov/director/quality_standards.htm, accessed July 11, 2007.

[8] Patterson D, Gibson GA and Katz R. A case for redundant arrays of inexpensive drives (RAID). *SIGMOD Conference* (1988). pp. 109–116. Also available at: http://www.eecs.berkeley.edu/Pubs/TechRpts/1987/CSD-87-391.pdf, accessed August 4, 2007.

[9] Weiner LR. *Digital Woes, Why We Should Not Depend on Software*. Menlo Park, CA: Addison-Wesley, 1994.

[10] Frauenheim F. Dell Drops Dome Tech Calls to India. Published on ZDNet News: November 24, 2003, 2:08 PM PT. Available at http://news.zdnet.com/2100-9584_22-5110933.html, accessed August 4, 2007.

[11] Gibson CF and Nolan RL. Managing the four stages of EDP growth. *Harvard Business Review*. January-February, 1974; 76–87.

[12] Verber M. How many administrators are enough? *Unix Review*. April 1991 (revised March 18, 2005). Available at: http://www.verber.com/mark/sysadm/how-many-admins.html, accessed August 9, 2007.

[13] Briggs B. I.T. Talent: In or Out? Internal Skills and Resources are Key Criteria When Provider Organizations Ponder Outsourcing I.T. projects. *Health Data Management*. March, 2002. Also available at: http://healthdatamanagement.com, accessed August 4, 2007.

[14] Cost-Effectiveness of Contracting for Services, Report 95-063. Department of Defense, Office of the Inspector General, Office of the Deputy Office for Auditing. December 30, 1994. Available at: http://www.dodig.osd.mil/audit/reports/fy95/95-063.pdf, accessed August 4, 2007.

[15] The cost-effectiveness of EDS service provision. UK Parliament, House of Commons, Public Accounts Committee Publications, Select Committee on Public Accounts, 28th Report. June 28, 2000. Available at: http://www.publications.parliament.uk/pa/cm199900/cmselect/cmpubacc/431/43102.htm, accessed August 4, 2007.

OPERATIONS AND SUPPORT

5

FROM PROJECT TO OPERATIONS: PLANNING TO AVOID PROBLEMS

WENDY GILES

UW Medicine, Seattle, WA

INTRODUCTION

Avoiding problems with clinical computing systems begins at the earliest decision points in selection, purchase, and implementation. It involves smart decisions to select software that works, to build and install it carefully, have good relationships with users and vendors, listen to their comments, monitor carefully to detect impending problems before they hit, expect and plan for downtimes, minimizing impact, and strive for best possible availability and reliability. Understanding the factors in preparation for and acquisition of a system includes looking at organizational readiness, and those elements of the acquisition process that support long-term success. Avoiding problems in the project phase requires attention to team structure and development as well as determining a project management approach. The implementation phase occurs over a project lifecycle including design, software configuration, testing, and training, described below. Although the information to follow has universal aspects, it is influenced by our experience at the University of Washington and is certainly not the only way to avoid problems. There are alternative approaches within each component and multiple paths to success of a clinical system.

We divide the life a clinical computing system within an organization into three parts: system acquisition, project, and operations.

During system acquisition, the system is investigated, selected and contracted for, or built. The project part of its life includes planning, building, training, and implementing. The operations phase is the ongoing use, maintenance, and support of the clinical computing system and its users, and is the focus of this book. However, the first two parts can determine success during system operations, and so we cover these parts too.

SYSTEM ACQUISITION

Before you can implement a clinical computing system, you must either acquire or built it. Today it is the norm for large medical centers to have or to be moving toward a fully electronic medical record (EMR[1]) and many factors are driving that move. To be successful, it is helpful to understand the factors at the front end of the process and how they will contribute to potential problems.

ORGANIZATIONAL READINESS

No system implementation will be without problems. There is ample evidence that large system implementations can take longer and cost more than planned and may result in frustration on the part of clinicians expected to use these systems. The organization *will* feel stress in some degree. Organizational leadership and staff must understand this and be prepared to persist through these periods. If the organization has answered the question "what will successful implementation and use of an EMR look like?" it will help in course corrections.

UNDERSTAND THE DRIVERS IN YOUR DECISION TO IMPLEMENT A CLINICAL SYSTEM

Awareness of the biggest drivers in your decision will help define a successful implementation for an organization and may lead decisions on order of implementing given applications. Drivers may include internal factors such as quality initiatives and external factors such as regulatory requirements, and each should be understood since they will shape both short and long-term vision and strategy for a clinical system.

---

[1] We will use the example of an electronic medical record (EMR) to describe this and other steps; the same points apply to most other clinical computing systems.

RECIPE FOR SUCCESS

Many factors will contribute to the outcome of an EMR implementation. In my experience, there are three key items essential to success.

1. *Organizational will* The road to an EMR will not always be smooth, and as noted above, will stress the organization at some point in the process. Changes in the industry and in the vendor landscape may lead to second-guessing of the decision to proceed or on the choice of EMR and other vendors. Clinicians who use the system will differ in their opinions and in their assessment of what makes a good system, and not all will be satisfied. The cost may be larger than expected and the functionality less than expected. Organizational leaders must have the will to stay the course or to make a difficult and potentially expensive decision to change course if it is clear the outcomes are not going to be met. Leadership is characterized by action during times of difficulty, more than it is by actions when things are going well.

2. *Clinical/operations ownership and leadership* A large component of organization will is provided through ownership of the system and leadership of the process by executives and operational leaders of the organization. They must set the vision based on organizational goals and support the operation as workflow changes. They help to ensure that it is a system designed for and used by clinicians.

3. *Information technology skill and experience* While IT cannot be the primary driver, it must be a strong partner. Infrastructure—network, servers, databases—must be robust, responsive, and fault tolerant. Help Desk and devices must work for the users, and security of data must be ensured.

REQUEST FOR PROPOSAL PROCESS

Embarking on an EMR journey will most likely start with the request for proposal (RFP) process, which is needed to select the best match for the organizations functions and needs. *Elements* of an RFP include an introduction of the organization, goals of the selection, and an overview of the process; functional requirements; mandatory technical requirements; and vendor considerations.

1. *Defining requirements* The functional requirements section should include a detailed query for features and functions desired, grouped by clinical functions such as documentation, CPOE, and pharmacy, with requirements for all disciplines. Technical requirements should be as

specific as possible and note any limitations or requirements specific to your environment. Starting with functional elements of the care process, the specific features needed to achieve that function should be detailed. For example, the function of physician orders would include questions on the ability to co-sign an order, how to manage a verbal order, and whether groupings or sets of orders can be built within the software. In addition to yes/no questions, it is helpful to ask for descriptive, more detailed information, such as: explain how the requirements of HIPAA are met, describe the types of expansion and enhancement options provided by design of your system, and briefly describe the system architecture of the proposed system that maximizes customization and system productivity.

Ideally, the RFP will be crafted by someone with a clinical background. At minimum, a group of clinicians familiar with the needs and requirements for a clinical system must be used as content experts and reviewers of the draft and final versions.

2. *Relationship to contract* Although not a formal contract, the vendor response begins to lay out the agreements being made and should be incorporated into the contract. Taking time and paying attention to detail in the RFP process is one of the biggest protections when expectations are not always matched by reality. If the vendor has responded "yes" to a given feature and upon building the system, it's not there, the RFP is the "evidence" and a form of commitment by the vendor. The vendor can be held to that commitment.

3. *Decision making* Once the RFP has been released and responses received, a process for weaning the number of respondents is needed. Determine a rating system to be used to score the individual responses, using individual scores for the major areas such as function, technical requirements, vendor considerations, and cost. Decide the minimum and maximum numbers of vendors to be fully evaluated. There may be several cuts to get to the preferred number, with vendors moving past the responses to an initial demonstration. It is recommended that the selection team receives the initial demonstration and has the ability to ask questions as a next step in the evaluation. At this point a further weaning to a smaller number should be done. Two and at most three vendors would be asked to do demonstrations to clinical users. This will minimize confusion about multiple systems and use precious clinician time more effectively. In advance of the demonstrations, provide the vendors a script of functions, actions and features to be demonstrated. Ensure time is allowed for questions. Develop a scoring tool for participants to rate the products and

distribute those as participants arrive. The final steps are site visits to comparable organizations using the software being considered. It is best to provide the site a list of objectives and questions to be answered during the visit. Once site visits are complete, references with other organizations should be conducted. At each step, a rating tool can be used for objective criteria in the decision process. The project selection team should be comprised of both operational/clinical staff and technical/IT staff. This group will make a final recommendation to the appropriate governance body, using a detailed report on the process, findings, and decision process.

CONTRACT NEGOTIATION

With a vendor now successfully selected, the contract negotiation begins. All organizations have people who are adept at contract negotiations and will now be pulled into the process; however, those people involved in the selection cycle are also essential to ensure the product and agreement will meet the intended needs.

This chapter will not go into specifics of contracting, but will share this author's bias that a deliverables-based contract is a good approach. It forces each side to determine what is needed, what they will need to achieve it, and immediately provides a collaborative relationship in which both sides are incented to work together to meet all milestones and deadlines. Deliverables-based contracts may be more expensive as the vendor adds a premium to cover what is considered additional risk, so a time-and-materials approach may be warranted for cost reasons. The challenge is to manage the vendor resources and hours to estimates. If the work is not completed with those resources/hours, then cost may be incurred in order to finish.

One of the most important portions of any contract is the commitment for system performance criteria. Specific performance metrics such as response time, availability percentage, and ability for maintenance to be conducted without downtime should be included. This, as well as the functionality, as described in the RFP should be included in defining system acceptance.

The negotiation process is the first step in your relationship with a vendor, and is an opportunity to set mutually beneficial goals and establish clarity of roles. Although the contract must address issue resolution and failure to perform aspects for both client and vendor, the objective is to never use these provisions.

BUDGET

Typically, a high level budget will be developed prior to the selection cycle and used for the decision to proceed. It will be progressively refined as the contract is negotiated, then as detailed project plans with associated resources are defined. Items in the budget should include investment costs such as hardware and software acquisition and maintenance, internal labor, and vendor and other external consulting costs. In addition to the cost of completing the project, life-cycle costs for maintaining the system should also be calculated and include the same elements.

PROJECT PHASE

In order to start the project, elements that must be in place are: project structure and organization chart, team members, presumptive budget, high-level schedule, and a project methodology.

PROJECT STRUCTURE

Project structure will include the strategic layer of executive sponsors and primary stakeholders; the tactical level of the team—clinical and technical—and its execution; and project management. As previously noted, the clinical/operational leadership is essential and should be steering project direction at the strategic level.

The project team will be a blend of skills such as clinical analysts who are subject matter experts themselves and who work with other subject matter experts; application analysts who configure and troubleshoot the application layer; and technical staff responsible for the infrastructure, including operating system, database administration and servers, and desktop and devices. Potential configurations include all staff working for the operations side in *an informatics model,* all staff reporting through IT, or a blend of staff reporting through both operations and IT. A sample project structure is shown in Figure 5.1.

BUILDING AND RETAINING A TEAM

Developing and keeping of a strong, capable team is one of the most important aspects in preventing and solving problems. The ideal team will consist of a blend of clinicians, individuals who know the

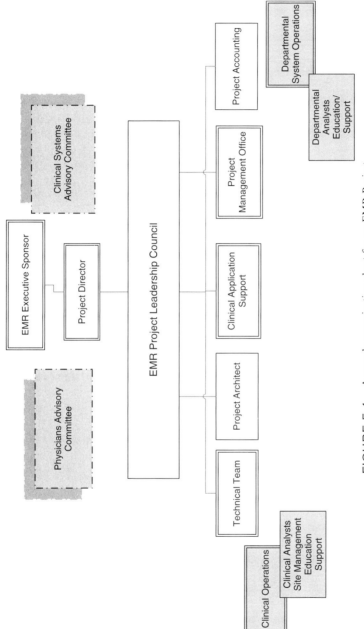

FIGURE 5.1   A sample organization chart for an EMR Project.

organization and its operations, and bright, innovative technical staff. The number of people on a team will vary based on the size and/or the approach used for implementation. If vendor services will be used to fast-track the design and build, the on-site team can be smaller. If a remote hosting approach is taken for the technical infrastructure, the on-site technical staff needs will be significantly less. For analysts working to design and build a system, there must be clinical experience in some or all of the roles. Individuals with IT backgrounds can make good decisions while relying on clinicians for input, but may not know all the questions to ask or areas for focus. The health-care environment is complex and challenging to learn; the right design decisions can only be made by those who know what is needed. Experience in the organization is not an absolute requirement but will support best possible decisions and will assist in implementation strategies, knowing characteristics of the involved units, workflow, and personalities. In addition to pertinent and recent clinical experience, the analyst skill set should include technical aptitude, strong analytic and communication skills, experience working in a high stress environment, and excellent interpersonal skills. It's hard to measure, but another desirable is the intangible of being able to "go with the flow" and diplomatically absorb the potential frustrations and anger of users with new workflow and systems.

Our experience has shown the need for two different types of analysts: clinical and application. Clinical analysts focus on workflow, design, and content optimization. Application analysts master the middleware of the application, including services, scripts, and application performance. This is a different team and skill set than the technical staff doing development and maintenance of the back-end operating system and database environment. The complexity of the software has been a factor, and it is possible with some systems that the analyst role can fill both clinical and application functions. Other organizations merge these roles into individuals who perform both clinical and application configuration roles. Having had this experience in the past, it can be very satisfying to use both skills. Increasingly there are programs in clinical informatics preparing people to work with clinical systems and will contribute to the evolution of new roles. It should be noted that the same staff will transition from development mode to an ongoing support and enhancement role. Helping them to prepare for the transition to this role must be considered. There is no single correct choice for how to organize the team for every organization; however, having people working closely and efficiently together with clinical, operational, and technical skills is key to avoiding problems.

Retention of staff is essential and factors which contribute include a challenging environment, reasonable expectations, competitive salaries, and the positive feedback loop of success.

PROJECT MANAGEMENT

A structured approach to any project is intended to ensure quality, and to support consistency and efficiency. The amount and formality of that structure may vary significantly within and between projects, based on the complexity of the software, timeline requirements, and the skill of the people involved. There are situations in which the need to be nimble and responsive outweighs the need to maintain strict project controls. Because of the scope and complexity of many clinical implementations, use of a formal project management methodology is recommended, with standardized approach to project plans, work breakdown structures, regular status reports, time tracking, and budget tracking. Routine assessment of percentage complete will help in managing to the schedule. Time tracking will link to budget actuals and provide a means to ensure adequate resources are assigned as well as to predict future efforts. Good project plans can support good execution. Elements of a methodology will include processes that address all phases as well as deployment. Items covered may include project charters and standards, workflow, requirements management, testing, training, and operational planning. Incorporating the project management functions into a Project Management Office (PMO) provides an umbrella function for project management activities. The PMO may be specific to a project or may be an organizational or IT-wide office. There are many excellent texts on standard project management to be used as a reference in setting up both a methodology and a PMO.[2]

IMPLEMENTATION METHODOLOGY—FOLLOW THE RECIPE

Software implementation follows a recipe and it is important to follow that recipe to minimize risks and prevent problems. Once the project kicks off, there are at least five distinct phases prior to conversion: plan, design, build, test, and train. Implementation of an

[2]Project Management Institute. A Guide to the Project Management Body of Knowledge. 3rd edition. Newton Square, PA: Project Management Institute, 2004.

electronic medical record will have multiple components, hence multiple project segments. Segments may be run fully in parallel, although some may need to be project managed separately, or may be run in serial fashion.

1. *Planning* The initial planning phase should solidify the basic implementation and rollout strategy and begin to build towards it. It is the period to focus on learning the new system, development of a detailed project plan, elaboration of the high-level budget, and finalizing the milestones and schedule. Learning the system in detail cannot be underestimated and it is the wise vendor who requires vendor-based training courses and certification prior to staff working with the system. Understanding the application features, what configuration decisions must be made, what is required, and what is optional are needed to drive the designing and building phases.

Another activity to be completed in the planning phase is a final project plan and schedule. Implementation support services, contracted or vendor-based, may provide assistance in detailing the tasks needed to complete a project segment as the project plan is built. Often the vendor will provide a template and may be contracted to complete the plan. Ideally, a project schedule is driven by the project tasks, their required duration, and the resources available, as detailed in the plan. There are certainly situations in which an implementation date is targeted and the project plan is worked to meet that date. That approach can work, but may need adjustments in resources, budget or both. In the traditional project model, the "three legs of the stool"—scope, schedule and resources—should always be kept in mind. An alteration in one of the legs must lead to an evaluation of impact on the other two.

Once the project plan is finalized and signed off, a project budget can be finalized and signed off. Any significant changes from the high-level budget should be brought to the attention of project leadership immediately.

2. *Design* The design phase has two components: process design and software design. *Process design* includes a thorough assessment of workflow and impacted clinical processes. It should be started by developing a detailed map/library of current state workflows, led by a clinician or business member of the project team. This can be a group process with clinicians as subject matter experts, or can be catalogued by a clinical analyst with in-depth understanding of workflow and the environment. Once the current state workflow is known, process change inherent to the new system and opportunities for change can

be determined, and a future state workflow is detailed. This is best done with a representative group of the clinicians who will use the system, who know the needs of a given area or specialty, and who are open to looking at systems in a new way. This effort can be done as concentrated sessions, running over 1–3 days or can be done with episodic meetings over a period of weeks or months. Clinician availability often determines the best approach. Redefinition of workflow processes is both a silver lining and one of the shoals of an implementation. During the process design phase, decisions are made which will impact the organization for years to come. Clinician agreement is essential. Because it can be difficult to move beyond "this is how we do it" to a new vision, guidance from consultants is often used in this phase. Conventional wisdom of not automating paper or mimicking existing processes is sound, but not always easy to see beyond.

Once the desired future state is cataloged, the next step is to use future state to design and tailor the software. This requires an analyst to translate the process design into the software capabilities. Familiarity with the software will aid immensely, although early in a project, this is often a challenge as the team may not have used or worked with the software extensively. The process group continues to be important in the *software design* process with ideas and designs vetted and agreed to by clinician representatives.

It may become apparent that the software does not completely support the desired workflow; the group tasked with process design will need to provide input on a best solution, with guidance and recommendations from the clinical analyst who understands what can and cannot be done with the software. Regardless of project size, capturing requirements as part of design will underpin and guide the work to follow. Within a formal project methodology, an official sign-off on the software design is often obtained from all participants, followed by completion of a detailed requirements document. The requirements document will detail scope and should be traceable through building, testing, and delivery. Some implementations may not have a formal document but will prototype design and go through iterative cycles of configuration until the design is finalized. The important point in avoiding problems is that design has been thorough and understood by all participants, and that it will support intended use when built.

3. *Building the system* Next is the build or configuration phase, in which the requirements are used to configure the system as it will be used. A detailed worklist is used to organize the activity and to support

task estimates for the work. Using the worklist/checklist and the task estimates, a routine (daily or weekly) assessment of percentage complete can be tracked. Now that the project team begins to work with the software, it may lead to ideas on how to better design. At the same time, requirements may change with new initiatives (e.g., Joint Commission requirements). Although the build phase is not the time to introduce significant changes, it should be recognized that there may need to be changes. The change control process can begin in this phase and be used to thoughtfully gate needed changes. As in other phases, a sign-off on the build should be obtained. Providing demonstrations to the design group as the build is occurring or at completion can be used to gain clinical sign-off.

4. *Testing* The testing phase is divided into segments, including unit test, application test, integration testing, performance testing, and user acceptance testing, which we define below. Underpinning a successful test is a methodology with detailed test scripts, coordinated approach to testing, and tracking of issues. Testing is performed to ensure that all aspects of the application(s) to be implemented, including interfaces, modifications, and peripheral devices, are functioning as intended. Of all the project segments, attention to detail in this segment is a must. Allow adequate time for the testing phase and begin preparation at the outset of the project.

Test scenarios identified from process flows and department content experts are utilized to develop test scripts that will validate the individual processes. Each functionality test is performed in a controlled environment. Staff members from their respective departments are called upon to utilize their real-world experience to identify test scenarios as well as to validate test results. See Figure 5.2 for the relationships among the primary testing components of a project.

(a) *Unit testing* Unit testing is the performance of tests on individual components for basic functionality within an application. Unit testing occurs during the implementation process, at the end of build. The objectives of unit testing are to test the database configuration/build for specific pieces of functionality within an application and to test that every item has been built correctly and is working correctly.

(b) *Application testing* After individual component tests are successfully completed, the collective application is tested for functionality. Application testing takes into consideration any

Test Level Relationship

Level	Unit	Application/Functional	Integration	Performance	Post Production
Description	Unit Testing is the lowest level of testing. Used to demonstrate that the application meets the requirements stated in the design specifications at the component/module level. It is a very specific test and is not intended to validate the interactions between components/modules	Application/Functional Testing is used to validate that the business and technical design requirements of the application have been met. This test helps evaluate system readiness by confirming that the applications function as intended.	Integration Testing is used to validate that the application or set of applications operate properly as an integrated set of products.	Performance Testing validates the ability of an application to function under maximum volumes and peak transaction loads. This type of testing also serves to validate the application under normal and stressed conditions supporting the application in the technical environment. Performance Testing can encompass both Stress and Volume Testing.	The purpose of Post Production testing is to ensure that the application installs properly and is stable in the production environment prior to release to the end user community.
Who and When	Who: • Executed by the Programmer or Software Analyst familiar with the application at the component/module level. When: • Usually executed as the first test for an application. May be executed after a fix or upgrade to the component/module.	Who: • Software Analyst familiar with the business and technical design requirements of the application When: • Executed after Unit testing has occurred. Application/ Functional Testing is usually the main level of testing and typically takes the longest.	Who: • Software Analyst familiar with the business and technical design requirements of the application When: • Executed after Unit testing and Application/Functional testing has occurred	Who: • Programmers, Technical System Analyst, and Software Analyst familiar with the business and technical design requirements of the application When: • Executed after Unit testing. This test should be performed as earlier as possible	Who: • Software Analyst familiar with the business and technical design requirements of the application When: • Executed after the application has promoted to the production environment.

FIGURE 5.2 Relationships among the primary testing components of a clinical computing project.

time lapses that occur naturally within the process.
(For example, if a radiologist must sign a radiology report
within 12 hours, the system needs to test that reports go into an
overdue status after 12 hours.) Application testing doesn't have
the depth of unit testing: for instance, not every orderable will
be tested. However, all logic is tested. So if there are five
variations of orders, one of each variation is ordered. The
objectives of application testing are to test that the database is
fully functional and to test the product from start to finish as
reflected in the future state process flows.

(c) *Integration testing* Integrated testing is the performance of
    tests on a collection of applications, external systems inter-
    faces, and interfaces for integrated functionality. All
    instances of data exchanges between affected applications
    and vendors are to be tested. Scenarios should reflect organ-
    izational processes as described in future state process
    flows. Integration testing occurs after application testing or
    whenever an interface is added. The objectives of integrated
    testing are to ensure processes and information shared across
    products perform correctly and to validate future state
    process flow designs as functional when utilized with
    patient scenarios.

(d) *Regression testing* Regression testing is performed to
    ensure changes made after installation of software fixes
    and enhancements have not had an undesirable impact on
    previously tested applications. The same test scripts for
    application testing may be used for regression testing.
    Regression testing occurs when software code changes are
    made in any environment (production, test, train, etc.). The
    objectives are to minimize the risk of making system changes
    by finding problems in test as well as to validate that code
    fixes function as specified.

(e) *Peripheral device testing* Peripheral device testing is the perform-
    ance of tests on peripheral devices such as medical devices,
    desktop PCs, printers, and bar code readers. It occurs after
    appropriate hardware is installed and medical device inter-
    faces and database build is complete. The objective of per-
    ipheral device testing is to ensure that devices work correctly
    with the applications.

(f) *Performance stress/volume testing* Performance stress/volume
    testing is the execution of scripts on workstations, networks,

hardware servers, database, and the host which measure performance. It occurs prior to conversion, after integrated and peripheral testing. The objective of performance stress/volume testing is to ensure that acceptable system performance results when system loads are increased beyond peak anticipated levels both for interactive processing and batch functions.

Each test phase has defined exit criteria and is not considered successful until all criteria have been met. After the successful completion of all testing, the project work team is asked to validate the findings and sign off on system functionality. After system sign-off, no changes will be made to the system before go-live.

None of the testing so far has occurred in the real world of production use, which means that unanticipated user activities or data may uncover problems. Piloting and first broad use should also be regarded as a test.

Software can be constructed and viewed as a structured hierarchy of ever increasing granularity. Software may then be tested by starting with the lowest level of granularity, proceeding up through integration and post-production testing. The progression of testing is as follows:

- Unit testing;
- Functional/application testing;
- Integration testing;
- Performance testing; and
- Post-production testing.

Testing levels have been structured in an attempt to identify, define, and promote organized, documented, and rational testing.

5. *Training* Planning for training begins early in the project cycle. An educational representative on the design teams will understand the context for how the system is to perform and the intended workflow when it is time to develop materials. While the system is being built, the training team can be defining objectives and writing training plans. Assistance with testing, beginning with application testing, is invaluable and will allow education resources to augment other project staff while helping them learn system function. See Chapter 8 for more details on training options at conversion and ongoing.

Training of staff signals the final phase prior to system conversion and the beginning of the transition to operations.

SUMMARY

From the outset of any clinical system implementation, it is important to have a mindset of forethought and attention to avoiding problems, and to spend time setting strategies and tactics explicitly to that end. Understanding the phases of the project, the elements within those phases, and how they contribute are an important start. There are strong bodies of knowledge in the areas listed above such as system selection, contract negotiation, development and retention of talented staff, project management, and implementation methodologies which can lend guidance, strengthen knowledge, and contribute to success. Success in the phases from initial planning to the pre-conversion training positions an organization for a smoother conversion and move to operations.

6

IMPLEMENTATION AND TRANSITION TO OPERATIONS

WENDY GILES

UW Medicine, Seattle, WA

INTRODUCTION

The success of a system conversion and the transition to operations involves careful planning of rollouts and their impact, attention to the details which support a smoothly running production system, and understanding and preparing for impact to business during times when the system is unavailable.

Conversion (also known as "go-live" or first production use) is the process of bringing the fully configured software live and available for use. It might be as quick as "flipping a switch" to bring all applications and all users live, or a much slower and gated process of bringing up groups of users over a longer period of time. Once the system is live for even a small group of users and is an essential part of business, it must be well maintained, available for use, and reliable.

Operations entails the day-to-day running, maintenance, enhancement, and safeguarding of the system to meet the availability and reliability requirements. In case the system will not be 100% available—planned or not—measures must be in place to allow clinical operations to continue during the downtime and to resume after it.

CONVERSION

PLANNING ROLLOUTS

How and when to convert to new software will depend on several factors, including number of users to be trained and who will be impacted; current state (for example, whether this a transition from paper to electronic or from an existing electronic system to a new one) and organizational tolerance for change. Careful thought must be given to staging of applications. Should they be implemented all together, in sequential fashion, or module by module? Should we roll out based on location, by user group, or by clinical function?

Approaches

A pilot phase is recommended for most deployments. Pilots are essential in large rollouts, but may not be needed for smaller changes. For an EMR implementation, a pilot of at least 4 weeks is recommended. It will test that the system can support the workflow, validate adequate training, and help identify technical and system issues. Allow time within and at the end of the pilot for remediation of issues, and make a go/no-go decision prior to exiting the pilot.

Once the pilot is complete, and the decision to proceed has been made, the full rollout begins. There are options here as well. A "Big Bang" will transition all users in all care areas to all or part of the new system. The primary benefit is there is no period in which care areas are using different systems, so the risks in transition from one area to another are lessened. A "Modified Big Bang" transitions all users in all care areas, but staggers the transition across multiple days (but not weeks). The staggered approach may be done based on physical proximity of areas or by logical work areas such as intensive care or perioperative. This minimizes the period with two systems and allows for fewer support resources to cover the affected areas. It can, however, be fatiguing as the level of intensity is sustained over a longer period of time.

Another approach is to roll out based on type of clinician. This typically means not all system functionality is being rolled out at once. Nurses may move to documentation prior to the physical therapy staff, or physicians may begin to document online prior to other disciplines. The support requirements will be lower, but the time period with multiple systems will be longer.

System function or application may also drive the conversion approach. Individual modules may be used in one department only. If there are modules for Pharmacy departmental function, only that area may be converted. Although there is impact to other areas or users such as nursing, that impact is smaller than if they were switching to a new system.

PLANNING FOR IMPACT TO OPERATIONS

During the conversion period, which requires "all hands on deck," an on-site command center should be established. This will be the central point of coordination for both technical and clinical support personnel throughout the conversion. Pick a central location, large enough to hold 10–20 staff; provide fixed network or wireless access points for computers; ensure adequate telephones; including a conference-ready speaker phone; and a large white board or easel. The command center will be staffed by analysts, application staff, technical experts, desktop, and Help Desk personnel.

In addition, there will be support staff, such as expert users, placed in each clinical unit or business area to provide real-time support. Additional support staff may be assigned as "roamers" to circulate to multiple areas and provide backup or augmentation for support. A central location for the user support staff adjacent or inside of the command center is also helpful as a place to hold shift change or group meetings to discuss issues or disseminate information.

Communication is extremely important during conversion to the new system. Multiple communication methods are needed for the core staff involved in a conversion. Options include e-mail, group and individual pagers, cell phones (which may not work or be allowed in some areas of the medical center), and conference calls. Group conference calls at set times can be established to review status, identify issues, and communicate information. There should also be the ability to quickly develop and distribute flyers and to use a phone tree to communicate quickly across the organization in the event of problems or the need for rapid education.

The length of time to keep the command center operational is dependent on the size of the rollout. A large conversion may need a 2-week, 24×7 command center initially, then scale back to 12 hours per day for an additional 1–2 weeks. Plan to keep the space longer than the planned conversion window in case there are problems. Be sure to consider and plan for a situation in which back-out or remediation is required. Understand the options and have a prioritized plan. Full downtime procedures for both clinical and IT staff must be in place prior to the conversion.

Any conversion will have problems and issues, and needs a process to capture them. An issues list format can be developed in advance. It should be assigned to one person to own, with secondary responsibility for off-shifts. Review this list on the regular status calls, assign responsibility for every issue, and track status closely.

Don't forget to provide snacks, beverages, and meals for the staff manning the center!

COMMUNICATION WITH THE ORGANIZATION DURING CONVERSION

A detailed communication plan should be in place prior to the start of conversion, with a focus on what and how to communicate to members of the project team, to the organization's executives, management and users, and to IT. Prior to the conversion, provide broad communication through multiple operational venues and methods to prepare the organization for the event and to set expectations. Consider a regular newsletter or flyer with a logo or color identified only with the project to provide information and updates to staff.

During the conversion, formal status e-mails or reports should be given to the executive and management teams for the clinical organization and to IT on a regular basis. Begin with daily or twice-daily updates. These can also be provided to the users, along with direct communication from support staff and any posters that provide updates and key information. Decide when the use of overhead paging is warranted, as well as when and how internal escalation and communication of issues is needed.

TRANSITION TO OPERATIONS

PRODUCTION REQUIREMENTS

Once the system has been converted, and running successfully for a period of time (defined prior to the conversion event and adjusted as needed), a formal transition to operations will occur. Planning for this during the project phase will ensure agreed-upon models for Help Desk, application support, and technical support, with corresponding Service Level Agreements on response time, time to problem resolution and expected system availability. Once a system is in production, staffing and on-call *must* provide 24 × 7 support. Plans for both expected and unexpected downtime should be complete and in place.

In addition to support, there must be a plan to accommodate system changes. Determine how the new application(s) will fit into established change control procedures: how frequently can changes be done, which changes require full review consideration, and which can be "fast-tracked."

Changes to the system will involve fixing bugs as well as ongoing refinement and enhancement. Outline a process to determine which elective changes will be made. User groups which meet regularly or existing meeting forums can be utilized for input and decisions. Decisions about content, format, and functionality changes should be owned by operations and facilitated by IT. Expect a tension between urgent requests and the need for careful planning, but remember it is essential that users know project and support teams are responsive and can trust changes will be made quickly.

DOWNTIME PLANNING

For either planned or unplanned downtime, the following need to be in place:

- Preferred communication methods and timing. Options include system pop-ups to warn the user to complete work and log off the system, banners that appear on every login, overhead announcements, newsletters, e-mail, or flyers.
- Policies and procedures for operations during a downtime cover what to do; the time frame before users should go to a paper-based system; and any policies regarding back entry of data after a downtime concludes. If no back entry is done, how is the gap in information explained in the record, with a reference to where the data is located.
- A downtime summary grid which details how each department functions during a downtime and provides contacts and accountable role for each department [Figure 6.1].

Category		
Documentation During ORCA Downtime	1.	Documentation is done on paper in an extended outage. Downtime packets are available in the Admitting Office at the discretion of the Nursing Supervisor/Charge Nurse. Guidelines for going to paper: 1 hour for ICUs, 4 hours for Acute Care, Psych and Rehab, 2 hours for LSU, 0.25 hours for PACU.
	2.	Access SONAR Device (PCLA Viewer) reports if downtime is extended. SONAR Device (PLCA Viewer) updates ORCA information several times within 24 hours until the time of the outage. Access Keys (jump drives) are located in the Admitting Office.
	3.	You will be notified if the ORCA Read Only Database will be available.
	4.	Providers may delay direct note entry until system is back up.
Medications	1.	During ORCA downtime, Pyxis patient lists and patient medication profiles will not be current. Patients admitted or transferred will need to be manually added to Pyxis medstations at the receiving unit.
	2.	Pharmacy will print the paper MAR when the decision has been made to go to downtime procedures. At that point medications will be documented on the paper MAR during downtime.
	3.	The paper MAR may not include the most recent medication orders. Confirm against the most recent physician order.
Laboratory	1.	STATS and critical values are called in to Patient Care Units.
	2.	Lab can generate results reports and distribute to Patient Care Units by tube, courier or fax. Call 4-3451.
	3.	Check Mindscape for lab and pathology results if available.
Allergies	1.	Allergy information can be obtained by asking the patient, red ID band, or SONAR Device (PCLA Viewer). SONAR Device (PCLA Viewer) updates several times within 24 hours until the time of the outage.
	2.	Look on Admit Orders to see if Allergy information was entered there.
Alerts	1.	Contact PDS (Medical Records) at 4-9009 for copy of Alert Care Plan if needed.
Radiology	1.	PACS and Mindscape are available for reviewing reports. Open PACS image to see report.
	2.	If unable to find the report, request a fax copy from Radiology. For ED patients call 4-3109. For all other patients, call Medical Records at 4-9000 to request a copy.

FIGURE 6.1 Portion of Harborview Medical Staff Inpatient Staff Downtime Quick Guide.

- Downtime packets: for extended downtime, include an overview of policies and procedures, along with paper forms for functions such as documentation or ordering

1. *Planned downtime* Downtime will be needed for ongoing system maintenance activities, such as patches, upgrades, and addition of new functionality. In addition to the items above, pre-defined downtime windows should be agreed upon, which impact a minimal number of users, ensure IT system staff are available, and avoid critical processing functions such as pharmacy fill lists or billing files. In most cases, this will occur during the night and/or on weekends.

2. *Unplanned downtime* When problems result in the system not being available and/or usable, downtime procedures are initiated. While focusing on resolution at the technical, network, or application level, initiate communication procedures internal to the medical center (user community) and internal to IT.

BUSINESS CONTINUITY

Business continuity is the ability to continue safe patient care during a period in which data cannot be accessed and/or entered. It is incumbent to provide a backup system and a failover system, which allows for reading or writing of data, for business continuity during downtimes. Elements to be considered for ensuring business continuity are

- What is the minimum number of workstations needed to access data in the event of a significant power outage? How many devices are on emergency power?
- How will or will data be available in the event of a network failure, when workstations cannot communicate with servers that hold the data? If a standalone system is in place for such an event, what data should be available on it?
- Should documents be available on paper in the event of an outage? Examples of essential data for patient safety include the medication administration record for each patient; a list of active orders; if CPOE is in use; and the most recent history and physical documentation.

At minimum, a read-only copy of the full data set should be available. And ideally, a failover system provides the ability to enter data and continue business, a "read-write" system. From the operations perspective, the decisions regarding going to the failover system are

- How long must the planned or unplanned downtime be before the read-only system is invoked? Take into account that a fail-over system may take from 1 to 4 hours to bring up.
- How long must the planned or unplanned downtime be before the "write" system is invoked? Take into account the alternatives for data entry and that time will be needed to copy the data entered back to the primary system.

BUSINESS RESUMPTION

Defined as the process of returning to normal operations once systems are fully available after a planned or unplanned outage, business resumption will be dependent on all interfaces being caught up, with no message queues, good system performance and stability, and users' awareness that the system is available. If the downtime has been lengthy, decisions may need to be made on whether to back enter data.

INCORPORATION INTO EMERGENCY MANAGEMENT AND DISASTER PLANNING

As the organizational dependency on clinical systems increases, incorporate testing of both business continuity and resumption into emergency management and disaster planning. At Harborview Medical Center, we've conducted two tabletop cyber drills as part of the annual disaster drills. The tabletop exercise scenario is an extensive, multi-day outage, and includes the opening of a command center and tracking of business resumption. In addition, a reference sheet in the disaster reference flipchart has been added for "Code Cyber," an internal system disaster called due to computer system failure(s), and reference links added to the intranet homepage.

SUMMARY

As with the project phases, the conversion and operations phases can be carefully managed with clear, well-thought-out strategies that help the users, the system, and the organization avoid problems. IT Systems are a necessary tool and resource for delivery of care in many organizations; as healthcare moves persistently to clinical computing, this primary dependency will only increase. Along with personnel and facilities, IT will be viewed as a fundamental piece of the organizational infrastructure and must be managed as such.

7

TROUBLESHOOTING: WHAT CAN GO WRONG AND HOW TO FIX IT

JAMIE TRIGG

IT Services, UW Medicine, Seattle, WA

JOHN DOULIS

Vanderbilt University, Nashville, TN

WHAT WE ARE UP AGAINST

SYSTEM COMPLEXITY

Keeping clinical systems running and available to users is more difficult partly because systems are increasingly complex. As the number and complexity of clinical computing systems rises and the need to exchange information between them increases, the computing infrastructure also becomes more complex and, potentially, unstable. An example of this complexity is the diagram below, which shows the vast number of devices and software "parts" (known as configuration items) that need to be separately configured in one academic medical center. The number of configuration items grew dramatically—by over 400%—in one year. Each of these items represents both hardware and software that must be configured and kept available for its respective user community.

Every component in the information technology infrastructure and their relationships are logged, tracked, controlled, and verified with emphasis placed on how these configuration items relate to one another.

Configuration Items
February 2007

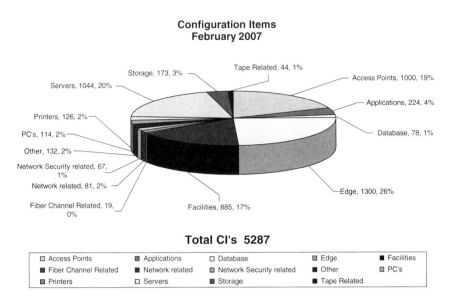

Storage, 173, 3% · Tape Related, 44, 1% · Access Points, 1000, 19%

Servers, 1044, 20% · Applications, 224, 4%

Printers, 126, 2% · Database, 78, 1%

PC's, 114, 2%

Other, 132, 2%

Network Security related, 67, 1%

Network related, 81, 2% · Edge, 1300, 26%

Fiber Channel Related, 19, 0% · Facilities, 885, 17%

Total CI's 5287

Access Points	Applications	Database	Edge	Facilities
Fiber Channel Related	Network related	Network Security related	Other	PC's
Printers	Servers	Storage	Tape Related	

Another example of clinical computing system complexity is the increasing need to exchange data between systems, in this case within the Horizon Clinical's infrastructure. This is predominantly a system developed by Vanderbilt's strategic development partner that forms the foundation of the Vanderbilt clinical documentation and order entry with combined clinical decision support. The diagrams below show the contrast between the WizOrder (also known as Horizon Expert Orders or HEO) architecture in 1999 and 2006. Due to advanced and broader functionality needs there is a stark increase in complexity between the two systems with a resulting increase in interdependencies of the components of the respective architectures. Many of these dependencies appear to be no longer necessary, but these dependencies make the infrastructure more complicated and unstable. In the last year, at least two incidents related to undocumented and unnecessary dependencies caused application downtime.

A third example is disaster recovery systems. There is a common misconception that disaster recovery can only help improve system availability when, in fact, it can actually worsen availability because they can add to complexity in the environment. We must first prevent source data loss through consistent backup and recovery, next prevent catastrophic disaster recovery situations where we would be out for days or weeks, and lastly reduce outage for services provided. Our strategy has been to address the "low hanging fruit" such

as poor processes or unnecessary downtime. We have been successful at reducing a large percentage of overall outages. We need to
understand that connectivity and resulting interdependencies are
now a leading contributor to outages. This includes the network,
storage area network, and firewall. Downtime is hard to prevent
because the infrastructure is made up of a series of intricate moving
parts all of which have to be available for the entire clinical computing system to be available to users.

Some of our first steps toward ensuring increased availability of
clinical systems will be achieved by documenting interdependencies of
our information system infrastructure.

Below is an example of the interruption in our CPOE (WizOrder/
HEO) application availability resulting from this increased complexity in just the year between 2005 and 2006. We classify "290" errors as
errors that the CPOE application servers have in either connecting to
their database servers or to the Generic Integrator Engine or to the
print sub-system.

System / error type	Duration	Total errors

WIZ
   "290" Errors
   (Print, Database, GIE)
	April–June 2005	0 errors for these three months

WIZ/HEO
   "290" Errors
   (Print, Database, GIE)
	April–June 2006	350 errors for these three months
		April – 204 / 146,447 sessions
		May – 88 / 218,381 sessions
		June – 58 / 192,070 sessions

COMPETING NEEDS

There is a necessary tension between the competing needs of developers, change/release management, and clinical end users who require
ever-increasing functionality. User demand for application integration drives us out of silos but at the same time increases dependencies.
As dependencies increase, so does complexity.

End users require increasing system functionality, which is
explained to the developers, but often in the form of ad-hoc requests
with few specifications and based on the limited or poor technical
applications knowledge of the requestors. Developers, keen to comply
with such requests, often bypass change and release management in
their quest to help the end user, who view change and release management as unnecessary bureaucratic hurdles. Unfortunately, this often

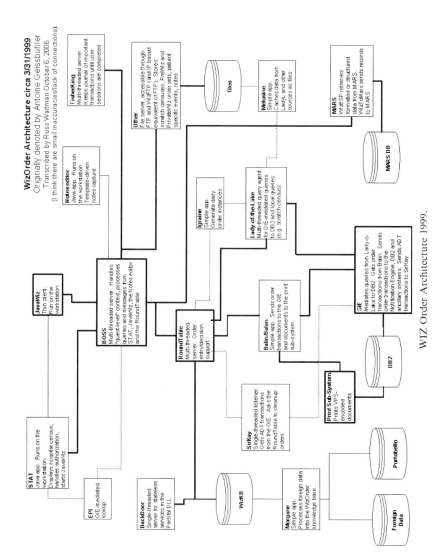

WizOrder Architecture circa 3/31/1999

Originally denoted by Antoine Geissbuhler
Transcribed by Russ Waitman October 6, 2006
(I think there are small inaccuracies/lack of connections)

FisherKing
Multi-threaded server. Keeps journal of important transactions until user sessions are completed

Notes editor
Java app. Runs on the workstation. Template-driven notes capture.

Uther
File server, accessible through FTP and WizFTP (an IP based equivalent of FTP). Stores scratch censuses, PreWiz and PrivateWiz order sets, patient specific events, notes

files

Melusine
Simple app. Caches data from LadyL and other sources as files

MARS
WizESP retrieves formatted or structured data from MARS. WizToMars sends records to MARS

MARS DB

Igraine
Simple app. Generate daily order instances.

Lady-of-the-Lake
Multi-threaded query agent for GIE-mediated queries to DB2 and local queries (e.g. scratch census)

JavaWiz
Thin client. Run on the workstation

BOSS
Multi-threaded server. Handles "quest-level" context, processes queries and messages from STAT, JavaWiz, the Notes editor and the RoundTable

RoundTable
Multi-threaded server. Order entry/decision support

Balin/Balan
Simple app. Sends order transactions to the GIE and documents to the print sub-system.

GIE
Mediates queries from Lady-of-Lake to DB2. Gets order transactions from Balin. Sends order transactions to the Notification Engine, DB2 and ancillary systems. Sends ADT transactions to SirKey

DB2

STAT
Java app. Runs on the workstation. Displays hospital census, handles authorization, starts JavaWiz

EPI
GIE-mediated lookup

BackDoor
Single-threaded server for stateless services in the Parsifal DLL.

SirKey
Single-threaded listener. Gets ADT transactions from the GIE. Asks the RoundTable to cleanup orders.

Print Sub-System
Prints VPS-encoded documents

WizKB

Morgane
Simple app. Processes foreign data into the WizOrder knowledge base.

Portobello

Foreign Data

WIZ Order Architecture 1999.

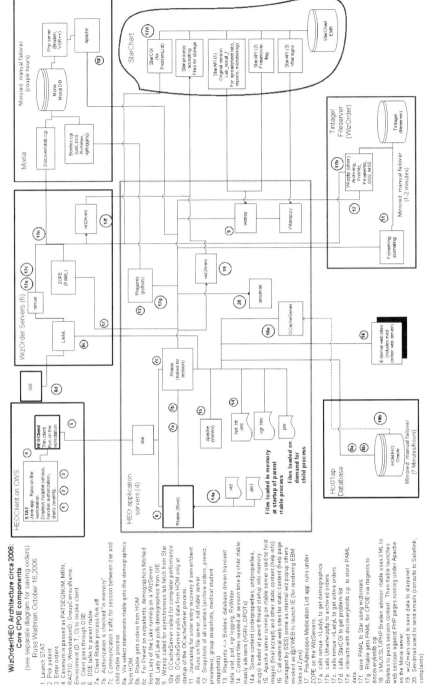

More complex WIZ/HEO Order Architecture 2006.

WizOrder/HEO Architecture circa 2006:
Core CPOE components
(see separate diagram for saving orders)
Russ Waitman October 16, 2006

1 Launch STAT
2 Pick patient
3 Enter orders
4 Casenum is passed as PATSEQNUM, MRN, RACFID, WorkstationID, GroupCensusName, Environment (D, T, O) to invoke client
5 Client goes through DSE
6 DSE talks to parent rtable
7a Client Rtable process fork off
7b Authorization is checked "in memory"
7c Communication traffic for session between dse and child rtable process
8a Via select statements rtable gets the demographics from HOM
8b Rtable gets orders from HOM
8c For Prewiz on outpatients, demographics fetched from Lady of the Lake running on a WizServer
8d Lady of Lake pulls demographics from GIE
9 Wizesp called for asynchronous lab fetch from Star
10a OCacheServer called for compelter performance
10b OCacheServer pulls data from HOM only at startup of the OCacheServer process
11 Journaling for order entry recovery if server/client die
12 Snapshots of all varieties (archive orders, prewiz, privatewiz, group snapshots, medical student snapshots)
13 Rtagents <-> Boletes: database driven transient data .usd, .psd, .vgr logging, RxWriter
14 Content files needed at session time by child rtable mianly advisors (VGRs, DPOTs)
14a Some content (ordproperties, untproperties, drugs) loaded at parent thread startup into memory
15 Apache server running on rtable server used to host images (final accept) and other static content (help info)
16 Call external web site for static content (help page managed by SSS) some as internal wiz popup others invoked as @XWEB to launch IE (for rendering EBM links al Zynx)
17 PreAdmission Medication List app. runs under ZOPE on the WizServers
17a calls nmue ->LadyL to get demographics
17b calls Uther/wizofp to archived orders
17c calls nmue ->LadyL to get active orders
17d calls StarCGI to get problem list
17e interacts with discoverylistdb.cgi to store PAML data
17f save PAML to Star using wizomars
17g Rtable gets PAML for CPOE via rtagents to discoverylistdb.cgi
18 XMLX/SLT/PHP Braden advisor. rtable uses XML to Boletes to pass session context. Then rtable launches web session against PHP pages running under Apache on the Moria server.
19 wriZImars used to save data to starpanel
20 Sendmail used to send emails (consults to Satellink, complaints)

introduces sudden change and unnecessary complexity to an ever increasingly complex infrastructure that results in downtime. "Change management" seeks to reduce such risk by offering a coordinated effort to obtain the proper approvals, authorization, and quality assurance steps to introduce the change. "Release management" packages these intended changes into release units to minimize disruption to the business. Release activities occur under the guidance and approval of change management.

RESOURCES: OPERATIONS, ENHANCEMENTS, AND PROJECTS

Further complicating this milieu is a lack of institutional standards and guideline controls, with standards and guidelines being perceived as restrictions rather than enablers. Standards and guidelines give direction in which creative energy can be channeled. Creation without direction can waste energy.

Sites should develop centralized policymaking and policy communications processes (for operational policies). This is an initial step toward breaking down silos that often and unfortunately exist between disparate information technology teams.

Current processes should be inventoried, modeled, examined for redundancy/duplication, and optimized. Process portfolios can then be created and distributed (i.e., made available centrally in an accessible and well-publicized manner), resulting in less duplication of effort, less confusion, and better overall understanding of information technology operations. A lack of shared vision and collective engagement can confound attempts to coordinate disparate teams to function without introducing unnecessary complexity into an increasingly fragile infrastructure.

Sites should have a set of concrete, well-defined goals that are known to all employees which will help increase system availability.

DIFFICULTY OF GETTING TO ROOT CAUSE: INCIDENT MANAGEMENT VERSUS PROBLEM MANAGEMENT

Often when faced with a significant outage that affects clinician users, an IT organization must focus on rapid resolution of an incident despite the fact that the resolution steps may reduce or eliminate the ability to get to root cause of the incident. The following is an example of a downtime incident that occurred to our CPOE system last year.

November 30, 2006 Incident

We had a CPOE application downtime, and while resolving the issue we faced a choice to either end the incident immediately and lose forensic evidence of the root cause or continue to analyze the problem and lengthen the duration of the downtime. We chose to the first option, to resolve the problem immediately. Since this incident, we have been unable to recreate downtime situation in our test system or even with assistance of McKesson's National Support services.

After much thought and analysis, we have identified one more area to focus on in an effort to get to the problem. If we can replicate the problem through these means, we can then try McKesson's diagnostic commands to see what's happening in the downstream systems. In this manner, we were looking not only at reproducing root causes, but also better configuration item mapping, better error messages to the help desk and support staff, and some quick customer frequently asked questions assistance in order to help in the diagnosis of root cause.

WHAT CAN GO WRONG (AND DOES)

One of the most important roles of clinical computing operations staff is to rapidly respond to problems affecting key clinical computing systems. In this section, we give several examples of outages and their impact on clinicians within a medical center.

PRESCRIPTION WRITING SOFTWARE OUTAGES

During the weeks of October 16, 2006 and October 23, 2006, our outpatient prescription writing application RxStar experienced repeated application freezes in production. Execute threads in the WebLogic server were fully consumed and the server became unresponsive resulting in 5 hours of downtime and requiring the team to bounce the server six to eight times.

Initially, we had several theories with a number of initiatives worked on, based on those theories:

1. Turning off threading for weight unless it is needed for dose checking.
2. Do not load RxStar (for shared session users over 375) unless they have used RxStar within the last month.

3. Turned off the SMTP service for sending e-mail alerts as a short-term measure—has RxStar gone down since this was turned off?
4. We discussed timing out the threading process if it exceeded 1 second (this was done after steps 1 and 2 are implemented due to the time it will take to implement)

What was the impact of these downtimes? Below we show the number of prescription written each day. Since October 16 was a holiday, we used the number of prescriptions written on September 25 to calculate the average. You can clearly see the impact that downtime has had on our prescription generation, not to mention the frustration felt by all the users.

Thursday, October 19, was the first downtime. Friday, October 20, everything worked as it should. On Saturday, October 21, a new release of RxStar was pushed to production.

Monday	Tuesday	Wednesday	Thursday	Friday
10/02: 1552	100/3: 1285	10/04: 1266	10/05: 1194	10/06: 995
10/09: 1506	10/10: 1237	10/11: 1127	1012: 1231	10/13: 1025
10/16: 1292 (HOLIDAY)	10/17: 1433	10/18: 1294	10/19: 696 (5 hours of downtime)	10/20: 1136
10/23: 792 (3 hours downtime)	10/24: 716 (clinic is not over yet 3:50 pm)—usage will be lower than average			

As a result of these downtimes, we lost about 1500 prescriptions being written in RxStar and, more importantly, we lost about two development days of working on the other initiatives.

On October 26, 2006, the team implemented a change in production to reduce the number of RxStar sessions. With this change, when RxStar is auto-started by StarPanel (our medical record portal), RxStar only loads data for the user if the user has used RxStar within the past 30 days. This change dramatically reduced the load on the RxStar server. RxStar CPU utilization, which previously hovered around 38% or higher, is now often below 25% and dips below 10%.

With the improved auto-start procedure, load on the RxStar server was now within a manageable range. However, as RxStar usage grows load will increase and we will need to migrate to the new OAS environment to take advantage of multiple clustered servers. We have also introduced server monitoring scripts, SiteScope, and Mercury synthetic user monitoring for data capture.

DOCUMENTATION SYSTEM OUTAGES

At Vanderbilt, cardiologists use a clinical documentation tool developed at Vanderbilt called Quill to generate the notes to document patient encounters in the cardiology office. It serves this purpose well, but has shown rather erratic behavior lately as our systems begin to have more complex interdependencies due to the increased need of interoperability. There are times it fails to save notes (which are fortunately retrievable later). There are also times that the program fails to open, which sends clinicians looking for alternative ways to document on the spur of the moment. More distressingly, the program sometimes stops working in the middle of a note. As you can imagine, this is rather awkward when one is in the midst of a busy clinic. At times, Quill was unavailable for use during much of the cardiologist's afternoon clinic. During other times, clinicians are unable to use it in the Cath Lab to generate Cath Lab Reports because the program fails to open.

As clinical end users are becoming rather dependent on these tools, reliability becomes a paramount issue.

On October 9, 2006, the Quill WebLogic instance became unresponsive many times between 10 am and 4:40 pm. When this occurred, the listen thread would not accept connections, and all RMI connections were terminated. After 5 minutes or so, the instance would start processing normally again. On the afternoon of October 9, we removed Mercury classes from the boot path and rebooted. The issue recurred once on the following day and has not recurred since.

At this point we've not been able to identify the root cause for the Quill outage. We have introduced server monitoring scripts in addition to OpNet, SiteScope, and Mercury synthetic user monitoring to gather more data.

CONTENT SWITCHING MODULE OUTAGES

The Cisco CSM device acts as a load balancer and port forwarding mechanism to direct traffic to our web applications. Since May 2006 we have experienced five outages of our CSM, resulting in downtime of applications such as the Workbrain nurse scheduling system, Epic & ORMIS terminal services, Nutrition Services, and Kronos. The average downtime has been 43 minutes. At Cisco's request we've modified the CSM configuration in an attempt to resolve these outages, but the risk of further outages remains.

All new applications and services, including the Patient Summary Service, will be accessed through the CSM. Therefore an outage in this component has the potential to cause downtime in many applications.

DATA CENTER POWER OUTAGE INCIDENT

On Thursday afternoon, August 10 at about 18:17, the hospital had an electrical hit from the storm that was passing through. Two hospital sites took electrical hits from the storm. This was a total blackout, hospital wide. Once the system sensed the power failure, and then started diesel generators the entire hospital except for emergency lighting was in total darkness for about 11–13 seconds. This 11–13 seconds was the time it took for the generators to start up and come to full power hospital wide (three Cat 1250 diesel generators). The hospital remained on diesel generator for approximately 15 minutes and back to electrical power from the public utility. There were no problems or issues in the data center. This shows that we performed well on facility power at the data center.

This incident points out two facts:

1. The many upgrades to the Vanderbilt University Hospital data center were worth the investment.
2. We did a good job of learning lessons from a prior data center power outage.

EXAMPLES OF OTHER PROBLEMS AND OUTAGES

In UW Medicine, our logs of clinical computing problems and system outages include network failures within and between medical centers, transient patient misidentification which could have created misunderstanding of laboratory results by treating physicians, loss of network connectivity for an entire medical center, air conditioning failure in a data center requiring temporary shutdown of many clinical computing applications, and many others.

HOW DO YOU PREVENT THINGS FROM GOING WRONG?

The process of identifying potential incidents starts before a system ever goes into production, with the initial system design. Because of physical, technical, and monetary restrictions, not all systems are brought up in a perfectly "bullet proof" state. An experienced technical architect will do their best to ensure that unnecessary system dependencies are kept to a minimum and that any required system dependencies are called out and monitored closely throughout the life span of the system.

System administrators should be keenly aware of all system dependencies and potential single points of failure, and should establish the necessary processes to monitor these areas closely, including the ability for the system to contact an administrator immediately should an established trouble threshold be reached on any number of different system metrics. Comprehensive documentation and monitoring of such potential trouble-spots allow system administrators to respond quickly when an incident arises and to more easily isolate the problem to a particular system component (e.g., network, server, operating system, database, middleware, application, etc.).

Once an acceptable and well-documented design is in place, the next level of incident prevention takes place at the system testing and user acceptance level. All clinical systems should be tested thoroughly, using a well-defined, comprehensive library of repeatable test suites, before they are relied upon in a real-life setting. Any potential "show stopper" bugs should be called out before a system is put into place, as once users are dependent upon the system it is much more difficult, time consuming, and costly to resolve the issue. While the ability for our IT organizations to meet project deadlines is important, the fact that patient safety is at stake with a majority of clinical systems implementations should be our primary concern.

It is important to note, however, that not all issues found in testing have the potential for impacting patient care and many application bugs may be worked around by modifying the processes that are used in conjunction with the system. System Test Managers and Project Managers should engage the appropriate subject matter experts on each project to assist in determining whether an issue is a true "show stopper" or if there might be a potential process workaround available.

In addition to application bugs, system performance should also be tested (performance testing is also referred to as volume or load testing) prior to a system being implemented. While application vendors may provide hardware, operating system, and other recommendations to support a stated performance metrics, such recommendations should not be relied upon solely to ensure that a system will meet user needs and expectations. Only actual performance testing can provide you with a true measure of what to expect once a system goes live. The advantages of the best application code will go unappreciated (and probably unused) if the underlying infrastructure cannot support the basic performance expectations of the system. Measured performance parameters should include speed of log-on, total time to access data, and total session time for one or more end-user workflows. There are a number of "automated" off-the-shelf tools that may be purchased to test system performance under anticipated end-user load, but meaningful system performance data may also be attained simply through a process of coordinating one or more multi-user testing sessions, taking the appropriate end-user timings and system load measurements, and then extrapolating them out to your anticipated production system load.

HOW DO YOU KNOW WHEN SOMETHING GOES WRONG?

Once a system is in place, IT organizations rely upon a series of system monitoring tools ranging from very root-level, targeted utilities such as nmon and sysmon that monitor for potential problems at the network, server, and operating system level, to application-specific tools built by clinical application vendors themselves that monitor and test very specific application components, to more advanced, comprehensive (and more expensive) monitoring suites such as BMC Patrol, Big Brother, and OpenView that can monitor for issues at the server level through the system middleware and even from an end-user or client perspective. Customized scripts may be written to monitor applications at the client and at the server level, with the monitors ranging from intelligent agents to open source alternatives.

While there are hundreds of metrics that may be measured for any given clinical system, system administrators should key in on a set standard of meaningful gauges that are monitored on a regular basis. Such standards include but are not limited to CPU usage, memory swap percentage, middleware throughput, end-user response time, concurrent usage, etc.

System software should be kept current by taking the latest system patches offered by each system component vendor (firmware, operating system, middleware, application upgrades, and so on) on a regular basis throughout the year. Regularly scheduled system maintenance windows should be scheduled on a regular basis throughout the year and should be incorporated into a system Operating Level Agreement between IT Services and system end-users. System Administrators should be careful to research any and all system patches for known issues before applying them to their own system. Optional patches or patches that are not applicable to your environment should be avoided altogether. All required patches should be tested thoroughly in a test environment before being applied to a production system. While it is good to be "current," it is not always good to be the first client on a given vendor patch (a situation that is referred to as "being on the bleeding edge"), as initial releases of such patches can, at times, be problematic.

Once a system is in place and an operational baseline has been achieved, it is just as important (and just as difficult) to manage system changes effectively in order to prevent the unforeseen circumstances of change. Changes are made constantly to every system throughout the entire system life cycle. Whether they are code changes being implemented as a result of changing user needs, additional servers being released due to increasing user concurrency, or code patches being released to prevent known bugs from occurring, one thing is certain—change will happen.

While change is a good and necessary part of any system lifecycle, change is also often an agent for system issues. Before any planned system change is made, it is important to understand how the system will be impacted by the change. Each requested change should be analyzed by an application architect against a system's current configuration (ideally, against a comprehensive Configuration Management Database or CMDB) in an effort to determine whether or not there could be any unintended negative consequences of the change. Once analyzed and approved from an architectural perspective, the change should be tested in a production-like test environment. Once tested, the change should again be reviewed prior to being implemented, this time by an application Change Control board, which is made up of representatives who support each of the various system components. Once approved by Change Control, the change is ready to go.

Change releases should take place during standard release or maintenance windows at times when end-user impact may be minimized.

Our normal maintenance windows are generally on Sunday mornings at 03:00 hours. Releases should be followed by a comprehensive post-release system validation process, which is comprised of a set of standard system test scripts. Users should not be allowed back on to the system until such validation has been completed. Following each release, systems should be monitored closely for potential issues. Due to the fact that changes are often implemented during times of low system use, problems are often not apparent until the next period of peak use or perhaps even later.

Despite our best efforts to the contrary, some changes that have been reviewed, approved, and tested will cause unanticipated issues to arise. In an effort to learn from our mistakes and prevent future incidents of the same nature from occurring, changes that are linked to such incidents should be subject to post-implementation review. For quality controls to be effective, however, the organizational culture must value quality assurance and support honest discussion of mistakes.

In addition to Change Control, a standard set of system metrics, often referred to as a system dashboard, should be established for each clinical system in an effort to plan for system growth and to look for patterns that may lead to decreased system performance and/or other incidents. At a minimum, system dashboard metrics should include overall system availability, number of concurrent users, average response time, and any other service-specific metrics that may be important to your organization (e.g. number of clinical notes written versus transcribed, etc.). Metrics for availability of a given service or application component should include outages, significant performance degradation, and service disruption. Availability should be calculated using total number of minutes available/possible on whatever interval is useful for your organization. For instance, at UW Medicine we calculate availability on both a weekly and year-to-date basis for what we see as the most useful availability representation.

In a perfect world we would always learn about incidents, well in advance of our users, via a series of finely tuned gauges and robots that constantly monitor and test our clinical systems to make certain they are in working order. Unfortunately, despite our best attempts, this is not always possible. Often we rely upon our user community to inform us of system problems. Users are often the best source of system incident data. The key to making best use of this valuable data is to make sure that you are gathering everything you will need to assist in troubleshooting and, eventually, resolving the issue. If a user calls to report an incident, it is absolutely vital to ask for the following data points: affected user, user contact info, when can we contact the user, a brief summary of the issue, whether or not the system is completely down, where the incident occurred, what type of client the user was using (e.g. PC or Mac? If web-based application, which browser? If Citrix, which server?), how long the incident lasted or if it is still occurring, and whether or not the issue can be reproduced. Ideally, we should not rely on our end-user community to inform us of system incidents, but when it does happen we should value the fact that the end user took the time to contact IT and make sure that we gather and use the information wisely.

Regardless of the source, all system incidents should be tracked in a single database source that allows for reporting based on certain operational factors such as application impacted, number of users impacted, length of incident, how the incident was reported, cause of the incident, related to system change, required follow up, etc. Standard incident reports should be produced regularly and reviewed for patterns. Often times, patterns can be identified through these reports that will allow you to recognize flaws in system design, problems with your change process, or system maintenance oversights before they become problems.

WHAT DO YOU DO WHEN SOMETHING GOES WRONG?

Now that you know that something is wrong, how do you deal with it? Even routine system disruptions dictate the need for standard diagnosis protocols.

Most incidents that are reported to a Service Desk are handled quickly and with little fanfare via level one (Trainers/Super Users) or level two (Service Desk) triage (for example, "My printer is not working," "I forgot my password," "I can't find the patient I'm looking for"). Such incidents usually do not suggest an imminent catastrophic system failure, but should still be documented for tracking and reporting purposes. There is a potential for such incidents to be related to an overarching problem and, unless we track the incident details, we may not get to the root of the problem.

Some incidents are not as easily resolved. Incidents making it to level three triage require the assistance of at least one system analyst to solve (e.g. "My regularly scheduled report job failed," "I can't find the document I was working on"). Incidents that are assigned to level four triage require assistance of multiple system experts (e.g. "The system keeps freezing," "I can't login to the system"). These incidents are generally of greater impact and may or may not be the precursor to a larger incident or an ongoing problem. Incidents requiring level three or four triage should be reviewed on a regular basis by a representative group of analysts and system administrators, who can look for patterns and conduct further troubleshooting in an effort to get to root cause. The supporting incident tracking process and/or system should be flexible enough to link potentially related incident reports to each other, as well as to a problem.

WHAT DO YOU DO WHEN SOMETHING REALLY BIG GOES WRONG?

How do we know there is a major outage taking place? Well, not surprisingly, in a clinical environment it's usually not too difficult— system operations may receive a page or an e-mail from one of the various monitoring systems alerting them to a problem; an analyst's computer screen may fill with error messages; or we may simply see a barrage of incoming calls to the Service Desk. There have been occasions during which we were not immediately made aware of an incident, but this has generally been because the impact of the incident was relatively low.

Once it's apparent that you're experiencing a major outage, the key to managing a major system incident effectively lies with your knowledge of your system, your ability to react quickly, and your ability to communicate with all affected parties. As mentioned previously, system dependencies and potential single points of failure must be documented clearly and understood by the incident team; response teams must know how to quickly isolate problem and rule out spurious data; and, perhaps most importantly, we must have the ability to communicate internally within IT, as well as with the entire impacted end-user community. Experienced team members with calm demeanor and strong leadership abilities are invaluable in these situations. Understanding the scope and potential causes of a major outage in a medical center requires a combination of a systematic approach and keen diagnostic skills.

During a major incident, the first thing that we attempt to do is understand the issue. Is it apparent what the root cause of the incident is? If not, can we at least isolate the problem to one or more system components? Do we have network connectivity? Is the application functioning normally? What about the database? Are there middleware problems? The easiest way that we have found to get to the bottom of the issue is to pull together a group of experts representing each application component (e.g., application manager, application analyst, system administrator, Citrix administrator, database administrator, network analyst, Service Desk representative) quickly and get them talking to one another.

The most effective tool that we've found for enabling this is a quick page sent to each responsible party with a teleconference bridge number for everyone to call into. We keep such page lists in synch on multiple file structures and the lists are transportable to any e-mail system that might be available at the time of any given outage; as a final fallback we can also page via phone. Once we have everyone on a teleconference bridge, we're usually able to understand the problem within a very short period of time. If we're not able to get to the bottom of things quickly, we escalate to the appropriate vendor(s) within 15–20 minutes.

An important note: One key point during this initial troubleshooting period is how quickly you can engage the vendor and get them logged in to your system. Make arrangements with your system administrators in advance to reduce all barriers to access for your vendors!

Once the problem is understood, we're usually able to gauge the true impact of the incident on our end-user community. However, there are occasionally incidents during which we are not able to easily gauge impact. In these cases, we also engage one or more end-user representatives via phone. This is usually the person who reported the outage or the designated site manager for each facility.

Once we understand the issue and the impact of the incident (this usually takes between 10–15 minutes), if the incident is in fact large scale, we're ready for a more comprehensive communication to take place. At this point, an Incident Manager is assigned and that person asks the Service Desk to establish a Major Outage call and they, in turn, page out teleconference bridge information to a wide range of people spanning IT Management, Clinical Analysts, and Clinical Administrators on-call. Some organizations use an Administrator on-call as coordinator of the Incident Management process, but this is not the case at UW Medicine. During the Major Outage call, role is taken, a brief summary of the issue is given by the Incident Manager, and an estimated time for resolution (if available) is provided. This call is also used to kickoff clinical communications and down-time procedures, if necessary. Occasionally, people who were not initially engaged in the technical teleconference attempt to use this call to troubleshoot the incident—these conversations should be deferred immediately to the technical teleconference. We repeat this process, having the Service Desk page out for regular update calls, hourly (or some other mutually agreeable interval), until the issue is resolved.

One of the keys to success with this process is that the Outage Call is separate from the Technical Call that is initiated shortly after the incident is reported. This allows the technical team to continue working the issue while the Incident Manager keeps everyone else up to date on their progress and the current estimated time for resolution, if known.

In case of a longer-term outage (an outage that would last longer than 8 hours), we have plans to staff the outage on shifts. Each shift would include an Incident Manager, who would transfer responsibility for coordination and communications of the event and corresponding progress via the above stated methods. Technical and clinical staff would be rotated in the same manner. Such a rotation would continue throughout the duration of the outage.

In addition to teleconference-based communications during a major incident, we also publish routine updates via our Downtime Communications e-mail distribution. This method of communication serves two purposes: It allows the people who have interest in the event but do not feel the need to join the teleconference call, the ability to keep abreast of the situation. It also acts as documentation and a timeline for incident postmortem analysis. We also post informational banners regarding the outage on all of our other major clinical systems. These notifications include a brief summary of the outage, ETA for resolution, potential workarounds, and who to call for more information. Following the incident, a formal Outage report is also filed and distributed to all of IT services.

A BRIEF INTRODUCTION TO INFORMATION TECHNOLOGY INFRASTRUCTURE LIBRARY

The Information Technology Infrastructure Library (ITIL) is a series of documents that are used to aid the implementation of a framework for Information Technology Service Management (ITSM). ITIL is important because it provides organizations with a pre-defined "best practices" roadmap for IT success.

There is a significant amount of documentation already available regarding the history of ITIL, so we won't get into that here. Suffice to say that ITIL is a proven framework that has been in use since the 1980s.

OVERVIEW

A high-level overview of the ITIL framework is as follows.

Framework

Service Support—The ITIL Service Support discipline is focused on the end user. The Service Desk (aka Help Desk, Call Center, etc.) acts as the single point of contact for the end users.

Incident Management—The goal of incident management is to restore system functionality as quickly as possible.

Problem Management—The goal of problem management is to resolve the root cause of incidents, thus reducing the long-term impact and overall risk to the organization. Once the root cause of a problem is properly diagnosed, the problem becomes a known error. As mentioned above, the goals of incident management and problem management may at times be in conflict.

Configuration Management—The goal of configuration management is to track each Configuration Item (CI) within an organization. Configuration items range from desktop PCs and printers to back-end servers and network and everything in between. In configuration management we track data regarding the current configuration of and relationships between each CI.

Change Management—The goal of change management is to ensure that standardized methods and procedures are used in the deployment of all changes. Such standardized methods are important in order to minimize the frequency and impact of change-related incidents and to increase overall system availability.

Release Management—The goal of release management is to protect the production system environment via the use of formal procedures and quality assurance tests. During the release management process we plan the release of new systems and system modifications, communicate with and manage expectations of the customers, and control the deployment.

Service Delivery—The goal of service delivery is a focus on world-class service to the customers of Information Technology. Service Delivery is made up of the following processes: Service Level Management, Capacity Management, IT Service Continuity Management, Availability Management, and Financial Management.

> *Service Level Management*—The primary focus of service level management is ongoing identification, monitoring, and review of the services offered by IT. Service Level Management uses Operating Level Agreements and other contracts to ensure that the agreed upon level of service is being provided to the customer.
>
> *Capacity Management*—The primary focus of capacity management is to match IT resources with customer demands.
>
> *IT Service Continuity Management*—The primary focus of IT service continuity management is to ensure the availability of IT services and, in the case of a disaster, rapid system recovery.
>
> *Availability Management*—The primary focus of availability management is for IT to provide an agreed upon level of availability over a set period of time. Availability management uses the following concepts: Reliability, Maintainability, Serviceabilty, Resilience, and Security.
>
> *Financial Management*—The primary focus of financial management is to provide accurate and cost-effective management of the assets/resources of IT services.

Security Management—The goal of security management is, obviously, information security. ITIL security management is based on ISO standards.

BEST PRACTICE RECOMMENDATIONS

ITIL Best Practice recommendations are grouped into the following categories:

> *ICT Infrastructure Management*—Information and communication technology (ICT) infrastructure management processes are best practice recommendations for the following IT services: Design and Planning, Deployment, Operations, and Technical Support.

Business Perspective—The business perspective is a group of best practices that attempts to address the issues of business continuity management, change management, and partnerships/outsource. This is also where the topics of IT Governance and Portfolio Management are addressed.

Application Management—These are best practice recommendations for the software development lifecycle with a focus on requirements gathering and management.

Software Asset Management—Software asset management best practices are focused on the infrastructure and processes necessary for the effective management, control, and protection of the software assets throughout their lifecycle.

Small-Scale Implementation—This section of ITIL focuses on best practices for implementation of ITIL concepts in smaller IT services departments.

ITIL IMPLEMENTATION

There are four steps to implementing ITIL best practices in a standard-scale IT organization. At a high level, they are as follows.

Phase 1—Stabilize

- Identify critical systems.
- Remove access to these systems; give minimal access only to a select few.
- Communicate change policies to those with access, and consequences of violation of those change policies.
- Set pre-defined change windows.
- Audit and very publicly enforce the policies.
- Be clear and firm about consequences for noncompliance.
- Audit live environments for unauthorized changes.

Phase 2—Understand the increasing fragility associated with increasing dependencies

- Inventory IT assets—find what is out there.
- Create and maintain CMDB.
- The CMDB must be *meaningful* and *manageable*.
- Find the systems that constantly break.
- Bring these systems under Change Management.
- Processes must be followed without exception, and eventually they will become second nature and will *accelerate* progress.

- Three of everything:
  - Odd numbers are more stable than even;
  - Three systems prevent outage if there is a large-scale failure.
- Active (not standby) systems: Active–passive is a waste of resources. All high availability systems should be active.
- Distributed computing:
  - As opposed to centralized (mainframe) model;
  - Many small systems.
- N-Tier architecture: Separate database servers, parsing, front end, application servers.
- Replication/geographic diversity: Data should be replicated to several locations (at least three) to avoid geographic disasters.
- Bypass capability: Should be able to route around problems for emergencies or maintenance purposes.

Phase 3—Create repeatable Build Library

- Make infrastructure and systems easier to rebuild than repair.
- DO NOT DO THINGS OVER AND OVER FROM SCRATCH.
- Identify and stock replacement parts.
- Create "Golden Builds" for fragile systems.
- Create Build Catalogs—everything necessary to rebuild a system from the ground up. Not a "point-and-click" level description, but enough so that the system could be recreated by a knowledgeable technical person.
- Establish release management.
- Be proactive.
- Fix problems, don't band-aid them.
- If something malfunctions, find the root cause and solve the problem.
- Equipment floats (spare parts pools):
  - Repairs should not be dependent on equipment orders/ shipping;
  - Spare parts should be on-hand.
- No single points of failure.
- No upgrading for the sake of upgrading:
  - Many systems are broken when an upgrade is performed, even though there is no compelling reason for an upgrade.

Phase 4—Continually Improve

- Manage by fact based on metrics.
- MEASURE.
- Use metrics to guide next project steps.
- Audit process compliance and configuration variance.
- Good metrics: Metrics must be *meaningful* in what they measure. 99.999% uptime is great unless the 0.001% downtime resulted in a huge financial loss.
  - Compliance;
  - Effectiveness;
  - Economy;
  - Efficiency; and
  - Equality.

Monitor

- Monitor at all infrastructure levels, network, database servers, interfaces, repositories, application servers, presentation layer.
- Detect issues before they cause service impact.

Implementation Focus Areas

Release planning: Lack of documentation at all levels— Documentation of systems is frequently outdated or non-existent. For example, one of our vendors is unable to provide database schema for system-in-production use, because it does not exist (they stated that they may have something that "is 90–95% accurate, but it changes so quickly that we can't keep it up to date").

This no doubt calls for the establishment of a formal Release Management system. A "golden code" release does not go into production until it is documented to the satisfaction of Operations. Operations place systems in production according to instructions provided in the release documentation.

Testing and QA Operations are mixed—This is alluded to in "Communications/Knowledge Exchange." Development and R&D activities affect production patient care systems. Developers provide direct support to applications, and have access to production systems. Resources are shared between patient care systems and research/development systems.

Development work should not touch production systems, and developers should never have access to production servers. Development changes should be handed to a QA team, which then submits the QA'd code along with appropriate documentation to Operations. Operations deploy changes to production when satisfied with the supportability of the release and completeness of the accompanying documentation. Change Management procedures are followed throughout the release cycle.

Post-Go-Live Monitoring—We have found that system monitoring is very inconsistent and often does not exist for critical pieces of infrastructure.

Deployment of standard monitoring tools throughout the institution is now a major initiative. Institutional monitoring tools should be managed by an enterprise monitoring group rather than individual system administrators, and the alerts generated by monitoring tools should flow to a centralized system.

Monitoring should be both from system and user perspectives. After monitoring baselines have been established, metrics on availability (from both an internal and from a user perspective) can be established, measured, and reported. This will allow the current system state to be documented, and for improvement to be measured on a forward-looking basis.

8

WORKING WITH THE USER COMMUNITY

PATTY HOEY

VA Puget Sound Health Care System, Seattle, WA

MATT EISENBERG

Children's Hospital and Regional Medical Center, M3-2 – Medical Informatics, Seattle, WA

> *The role of today's physician executive is one of the most challenging and rewarding jobs in medicine. The good news is that most physicians are not fighting to take your job; the bad news is there's a reason. Your satisfaction will not come from the thankful patient following a successful operation but from the quiet knowledge that your leadership has made the hospital a safer, more efficient place for many and that your leadership has played a small part to align the incentives of the medical staff with those of the hospital. In today's health care crisis, physicians and hospital administrators must work together to solve the myriad of economic and quality problems. The words of Ben Franklin have never been more relevant. "We must hang together or we shall surely all hang separately."*
>
> *Robert W. Chappell Jr., MD, MBA*
> *Physician Executive, 2004*

Numerous studies have described the barriers and keys to successful electronic medical record (EMR) implementation, many focusing on computerized provider order entry (CPOE). Ash and colleagues have identified several elements including time considerations, meeting informational needs, integration into workflow, essential people, institutional trust, and improvement through evaluation including paying attention to user feedback [1]. Reed Gardner has summed it all up by suggesting "what we are doing is 90% social and political and only about 10% technology" [2]. Even if you've already managed to engage your user community as part of a successful, highly visible EMR or CPOE implementation, you will need to work even harder to maintain that partnership between busy clinician users and your information services departments.

To support and expand existing functionality, to keep up with software upgrades as well as new medical knowledge and to respond to the constant institutional pressures to streamline the care process and reduce waste, you must crystallize and sustain previous successful efforts used during the initial design, build, test, train, and implement project cycle. This chapter will focus on the experience of two large tertiary-care medical centers with very different patient populations during the post-implementation phase of their conversions from paper-based charts to EMRs.

SETTINGS AND IMPLEMENTATION HISTORY

VA Puget Sound is comprised of two divisions in Seattle and Tacoma, Washington, and a system of community-based outpatient clinics serving American veterans which together have more than 600 000 outpatient visits and more than 8300 inpatient discharges annually. The combined medical centers have 504 beds with an average daily census of 368. The Seattle division, where 511 residents in many specialties, more than 60 medical students, and 1600 allied health students train each year, is a major teaching hospital of the University of Washington. VA Puget Sound uses CPRS, the computerized patient record system developed by the Department of Veterans Affairs, which integrates direct provider order entry, note entry, results review, image display, decision support, and access to patient data at any VA or Department of Defense facility with pharmacy, imaging, laboratory, dietetics, scheduling, vital signs, nursing, and barcode medication administration programs. CPRS implementation began in 1996 with the acceptance of VA Puget Sound as a national test site for CPRS development, and the subsequent creation of a new department, Clinical Information Management, aligned under the office of the Medical Director. Implementation occurred in phases spaced several weeks apart, beginning with the nursing homes, continuing with the inpatient wards and intensive care units, and culminating with the outpatient clinic network. CPRS is now uniformly used nationwide throughout the VA system, and current work focuses on secure, seamless integration of clinical information between VA facilities and with other federal and state agencies. In 2004 the nation-wide CPRS network incorporated over 1.25 billion orders, 599 million documents, and 246 million images. Over 565 million medication administrations were documented through the bar code medication administration process.

Seattle Children's Hospital and Regional Medical Center is a 250-bed, tertiary-care hospital that is part of the WWAMI region and affiliated with the University of Washington. The medical center has approximately 11 000 inpatient admissions per year, performs 10 000 surgical cases, and sees 40 000 ED visits and approximately 175 000 outpatient pediatric subspecialty visits per year. Active medical staff includes both community physicians and University of Washington faculty, as well as 750 residents who work at the institution each year for varying lengths of time. Children's embarked on the road to an EMR several years ago in the belief that it would directly improve the quality and safety of the care provided. This clinical database would also allow the medical center to analyze the quality and cost effectiveness of care and dramatically expand clinical research capabilities. During the initial phase, the medical center implemented results reporting on a Cerner Millennium platform version 7.8 in July 2002 including demographic data, visit data, laboratory data, radiology reports, and dictated documents. These were available from any computer in the hospital system as well as through a secure web portal. Phase two included CPOE implemented in all inpatient and emergency department areas in November of 2003 as part of a hospital patient safety initiative. Phase three included ambulatory CPOE in June 2006 in over 30 subspecialty clinics. Although dictated reports are interfaced into the EMR, direct online documentation was limited. The Hematology–Oncology care program has all of its documentation online in text format. Future phases include enterprise-wide online documentation with the goal of maximizing structured data element documentation, potentially using a multi-contributor model. In addition, the medical center will be implementing enterprise wide digital scanning, hospital-wide interactive flow sheet documentation that supports BMDI data extraction, and additional integrated applications for emergency and surgical services. Pharmacy and radiology information systems are integrated (Cerner Millennium) and the laboratory information system is an older Cerner application. PACS, ADT, and scheduling applications are non-integrated applications. The medical center averages approximately 2000 users per day with 10–20 000 new orders entered per day.

LEADERSHIP AND INSTITUTIONAL
FOUNDATIONS

Institutional leadership and an explicit, obsessive commitment to improving patient safety and the quality of care are essential. Technology should be seen as a powerful tool in any institution's armamentarium of quality and safety improvement. Each implementation project should be seen as part of an integrated, phased, long-term information technology vision. Leaders should use real examples of illegible prescriptions and medication errors to engage staff. All levels of administrative and clinical leadership must become active champions to build and sustain your EMR. This includes Board membership and the entire C-suite of administration. During implementation and beyond, many existing policies and procedure will need to me modified and new policies created to cover many topics including but not limited to CPOE, critical result reporting, downtime/uptime procedures.

It is useful to identify and engage opinion leaders and early adopters amongst your clinical leadership as soon as possible. Typically, these busy clinicians are in great demand. They may be willing to assist with developing or reviewing clinical content, describing the current state workflow and communicating with/to colleagues. It is critical that institutional leadership acknowledge their work and time both professionally and financially.

At the operational project level, solid project management that includes clear scope and achievable timelines is also essential. Resource allocation at critical times along the way is always a challenge. At Seattle Children's, during its CPOE implementation project regular "War Room" meetings were set up with executive sponsors and project managers. Needs for additional IS analyst and clinical resources to complete project goals were identified and met immediately to make sure project timelines were met. After implementation, this becomes even more challenging. At Seattle Children's, workgroups with identified departmental champions are being established who will regularly review content and inform the information management team of current and future state workflows. Adequate staffing for both production support/maintenance and additional new projects must be budgeted appropriately.

At VA Puget Sound, senior management likewise committed significant resources to recruiting clinical and technical personnel and for the hardware and infrastructure needed for a large-scale implementation. Their active and visible support in written communications, at institutional meetings, and even making rounds in clinical areas during the height of the implementation effort, was crucial to our success. A CPRS Steering Committee was established, with membership comprised of clinical service line leaders, "clinical champions," and the Medical Director, which reported to the facility's Clinical Executive Board and continues to do so. Clinical champions were the clinical opinion leaders who served to positively influence the attitudes of their peers and staff towards the system, provide front-line experience to the clinical information team for continuous improvement, and on occasion, informally serve in a "super user" capacity. After implementation, support from senior management is still important, but resource and personnel allocation is accomplished through more routine, committee-based mechanisms. The CPRS Steering Committee continues to meet monthly with the Medical Director and clinical leadership to address new informatics initiatives and opportunities.

COMMUNICATION

Communicating change to a large organization is challenging. There is no single communication tool that will effectively reach your entire user community. Organizational structure, shift work, basic computer skill level, and other personal and organizational preferences will make it easier or harder for some users to access e-mail, voicemail, snail-mail, web sites, in-person presentations, peer-to-peer networking or "information alerts" posted as part of your EMR. At Seattle Children's, the approach has been to employ multiple communication tools in the hope of reaching the widest possible audience. During the late stages of project implementation, when there is focused institutional attention, it is somewhat easier. However, all too frequently, information overload begins to impact the ability of the implementation team to communicate with its target audience. It is essential to clearly identify what news "is fit to print" and what changes can easily be incorporated into the existing user workflow. Some information may be more successfully targeted to a defined subset of your user community.

At Seattle Children's, the information management team relies heavily on face-to-face meetings for communication. EMR issues are addressed at all departmental meetings, new staff orientations, pertinent educational rounds and teaching sessions as well as community provider meetings. The intranet is used for announcements via Children's "In House" online magazine, and includes a regular section on scheduled downtimes that may impact the clinical areas. E-mail "Central Broadcasts" for time- critical issues and a Clinical Information Systems Communication e-mail that is sent to our entire user community for less time-critical updates are both employed. Information is posted on the resident education web site and EMR changes that affect the residents are often included in their weekly resident updates.

Print materials include letters and news bulletins to the user community and beyond. In the days when staff still received pay stubs by mail, periodic updates on EMR projects were included with pay stubs. Small informational flyers are very effective, particularly when strategically posted in busy clinical areas such as staff bathrooms. The team typically expands the usual "Pardon Our Dust" poster notification throughout the hospital aimed at patients as well as staff during any new implementation. "How to" guides and tri-folded "job aids" are liberally dispensed to staff during orientation and with new initiatives.

At VA Puget Sound, communication with users is accomplished with formal policies and procedures, new staff orientations, pre-scheduled training sessions, staff meetings in the form of a formal agenda item or an open-forum "IT minute" at the end of the agenda, e-mail bulletins, posters in staff conference rooms and break rooms, printed handouts and pocket-cards, links on the medical center's internal web site to bulletins and interactive web videos, "IT rounds," and with cross-membership of the clinical information team in facility oversight committees. During computer downtime, overhead announcements are made by the hospital operators according to a protocol involving network managers and the clinical information team to keep staff apprised. When downtime occurs at night, to avoid disturbing patients' sleep, communication between the information systems service and the front-line staff occurs via the Administrative Officer of the Day and the Nursing Officer of the Day, and by pager and phone. Internally, members of the team communicate by e-mail, weekly meetings, and for time-sensitive matters, by text pager. As the agency integrates and standardizes computer operations more and more across the nation, communication with regional network managers and clinical information teams at other VA medical centers has become critical to daily operations and necessitated delineation of protocols and service level agreements.

STANDARDIZING THE CARE PROCESS

Your EMR may be one of the most effective means of standardizing the health-care delivery process in the hopes of improving guideline compliance and ultimately, improved patient outcomes. Development of standards for the design and constructions of medication order sentences, standardized medical infusions, condition or procedure based order sets, and online clinical documentation will be important both to assist implementation and to help with the creation of new and maintenance of existing clinical content.

At Seattle Children's, key improvements in the medication delivery process and clinical decision support tools were incorporated into the EMR that had an immediate impact patient safety. An online pediatric formulary was developed that is updated for all drugs available for inpatient CPOE. "Order sentences" and dose range checking parameters that exactly matched the online prescribing information were created. A standard set of medications drips was created with a drip table that calculated rates to be used with pre-programmed smart pumps. The clinical information systems team is represented on the hospital Pharmacy and Therapeutics Committee so that newly approved medications can be easily added to the EMR with simultaneous updates to the online formulary.

At VA Puget Sound, an extensive compendium of order menus, order sets, quick orders, note templates, and clinical reminders are maintained by the clinical information management team with hyperlinks to clinical guidelines, calculators, patient handouts, and other tools. During implementation, the rush to provide these tools to the eager user community occasionally resulted in less than rigorous evaluation and too much customization. The benefits of uniform protocols, aggregated data, and economies of scale with respect to the building blocks of the information system were overlooked. Evidence-based standards and a systematic approval process for all of these tools were subsequently established. The information management team also has cross-representation on the Pharmacy and Therapeutics Committee, Security and Confidentiality Committee, and other oversight committees to support patients and clinical users in a uniform and systematic manner.

UNDERSTANDING WORKFLOW

Information systems analysts must have an understanding of the procedures and culture of the working environment. Those with clinical backgrounds must maintain credibility by demonstrating and maintaining clinical competencies. At Seattle Children's, a multidisciplinary approach is used that incorporated physicians, nurses, pharmacists, diagnostic ancillary staff (Lab, Radiology, Cardiodiagnostics, Neurodiagnostics), therapeutic ancillary services (PT, OT, Speech, Social Services, Child life service) as well as scheduling and business services representatives. During the project phase, regular multidisciplinary workgroups we call "COWS" were instituted. This was an acronym for Clinical Operations Workgroups. During these sessions, design options based on software functionality were reviewed with some basic analysis including identified pros and cons of the design. Additional issues were identified and through consensus, future state workflow designs were established. After implementation, this group was converted to a standing hospital committee, the Clinical Systems Review Board, that serves as a clinical oversight group for new functionality and workflow issues.

One key element of workflow for busy clinicians is that the care process is a 24-hour, 7-days-a-week process and clinicians must easily access the EMR from home and outside the institution. At Seattle Children's, an easily accessible web-based portal was established that could be accessed from any place internet access was available but requiring both network and CIS application authentication. There were some challenges ensuring users' home computers and networks were safe, so standards were established and published. Other challenges were faced relating to the variability in hardware, software, and operating systems that were used by our active staff.

At VA Puget Sound, clinical information systems analysts are called Clinical Applications Coordinators, or "CACs." It was recognized that these individuals bridge two worlds, the clinical and technical, and should possess certain characteristics from both environments. Initially, internal candidates were desired who understood local processes, organizational culture, and could utilize prior professional relationships to facilitate the implementation in sometimes hostile situations. However, as the transition progressed over time from a paper-based medical record to an electronic record that increasingly included auxiliary systems for decision support, telemedicine, interfacility consulting, etc., the fresh perspective introduced by external

CAC candidates from other VA facilities and from the private sector also proved invaluable. Technical abilities, training experience, speaking and writing skills, troubleshooting skills, empathy, self-motivation, and a systems perspective are deemed desirable traits of effective CACs, whether "home-grown" or recruited from other facilities.

Cross-membership of these analysts in key oversight committees within the medical center helps the clinical information team discover and help resolve problems through integrated application of computerized solutions. Problems long hidden by the limitations of paper-based records become glaringly apparent during implementation, and new opportunities are elucidated. For these reasons, clinically experienced CACs well-versed in the procedures and culture of the organization are regarded to be assets both to the implementation effort, and to the new rapid learning environment. These committees include

- CPRS Steering Committee;
- Pharmacy and Therapeutics Committee;
- Templates/Titles Committee (formerly "Forms Committee");
- Clinical Reminder Committee;
- Order Set/Guidelines Committee;
- Security and Confidentiality Committee;
- Contingency Planning Committee;
- Aggregated Medication Error Committee; and
- Regional and National VA CAC Committees.

TRAINING

At Seattle Children's, initial training for results reporting was limited to job aids and online manuals. For inpatient CPOE training tools were developed including customized, role-specific, web-based training (WBT) tools. WBT was used in conjunction with scenario-based classroom training. Physicians were required to complete 2–3 hours of training, half of which included the WBT and rest included role-specific scenarios and an opportunity to practice in a training environment. Nurses and ancillary clinical staff were required to complete 4 hours of training which combined the WBT with more specific role-based scenarios. Identified super users functioned as teaching assistants during the training. For ambulatory CPOE ALL 1000 users attended 4 hours classroom session over 5 weeks AFTER completing a 1 hour fundamental WBT session and an optional WBT for provider electronic prescribing.

Users were asked to volunteer to be part of the super user community before each implementation. Surprisingly, volunteers came from a variety of different technical competencies. Some expert computer users wanted to lead the way while others who clearly felt their basic computer skills lacking hoped that involvement in the super user group would give them more time to "face their computer phobias" head on. Simple exercises were created for super users that they could practice in a training environment. During classroom training, super users acted as teaching assistants. By teaching others, they solidified their skills. During implementation, super users were used as active parts of our transition teams or work group specific assistants. During the ambulatory CPOE implementation, 10 full time clinical super users were paid for 2 weeks to support other clinicians. After implementation, monthly super user meetings of the super user network (SUN) are held, led by an information systems liaison analyst–nurse. These meetings are used as a regular bi-directional way to update users on enhancements and upgrades as well as getting additional enhancement request, review and testing of new functionality and further input on workflow impact.

The changing nature of clinical staff is a reality in all institutions but it's particularly acute in teaching hospitals. At Children's hospital, there are 75 full time pediatric resident positions but over 750 residents from the University of Washington and elsewhere rotating into the hospital every year. Residents must "arrive prepared to begin clinical work" and this can be a real challenge, particularly since many come from institutions where CPOE has not been implemented or their basic EMR is remarkably different in the user interface. Residents and new physicians and mid-level providers are now given access to the WBT tools BEFORE they arrive on-site and we track their compliance. Active user names and passwords are distributed after completion of the WBT. An annual orientation is conducted for our core pediatric residents during their orientation which includes a series of tips and tricks. Peer-to-peer learning and super user assistance are the main source of "how to" information. Access is provided to an online catalog of "how to" help tools that can be launched directly from within the EMR. Nursing and ancillary staff continue to attend classroom training delivered by our IS training team. They all complete an initial mentored transition that adds additional on-the-job training as they are oriented to their clinical duties.

Transient or infrequent users such as community surgeons who only use Seattle Children's hospital four or five times a year and a limited number of computer-phobes continue to be a challenge. Peer-to-peer assistance is offered, either by appointment or on demand from one of the physician informaticians or the nurse analyst liaison. As part of all of implementation projects, users were asked who felt that they lacked some of the basic computer knowledge to identify themselves. We also looked to peers and administrators to identify users who we knew would need additional training and on-going support. One-on-one sessions are available to anyone as needed and additional super user or colleague support during the actual implementation.

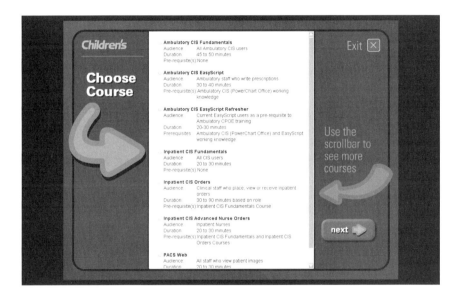

At VA Puget Sound, CPRS training during the implementation phase involved groups of 20 users in classrooms with several instructors, and lasted 4–8 hours. Regularly scheduled drop-in tutorial sessions were also scheduled from noon to 1 pm, so that users with specific questions could come to the training room during their lunch break and receive help. As the baseline level of user skill increased and the software matured, the training program, formerly conducted by CACs, evolved into smaller group training sessions, a shorter curriculum, varied locations, and came increasingly under the jurisdiction of the clinical bed services. University of Washington resident physicians are currently trained in 90-minute classroom sessions during the first morning of their rotation by Team Assistants who are employed by the clinical service lines and serve an administrative support role for the resident teams. New nurses and nursing students are trained by a staff of four nurse CACs in classroom settings. A "super user" program utilizing self-nominated, service-line-approved, CAC-trained front-line staff is particularly helpful in embedding advanced CPRS skills amongst the user community, especially during non-business hours when institutional support is decreased. Informal peer training now plays a significant support role, but in the early phases depended on a critical mass of skilled users being available. In addition, six-minute, professionally produced, interactive, WBT modules are offered describing CPRS features which are available within and outside the VA firewall (Figure 8.1), as well as printable pocket guides. These serve to augment classroom training and to document the staff's competency in using CPRS. Other automated training tools that are being developed include web pages and pod casts embedded within CPRS itself, which provide basic skills training as well as clinical advice and guidelines. CACs often provide short, specific training on new initiatives at drop-in lunch-and-learn sessions and at "IT minutes" added to the agenda of department meetings. Daily CAC rounds provide busy front-line users an

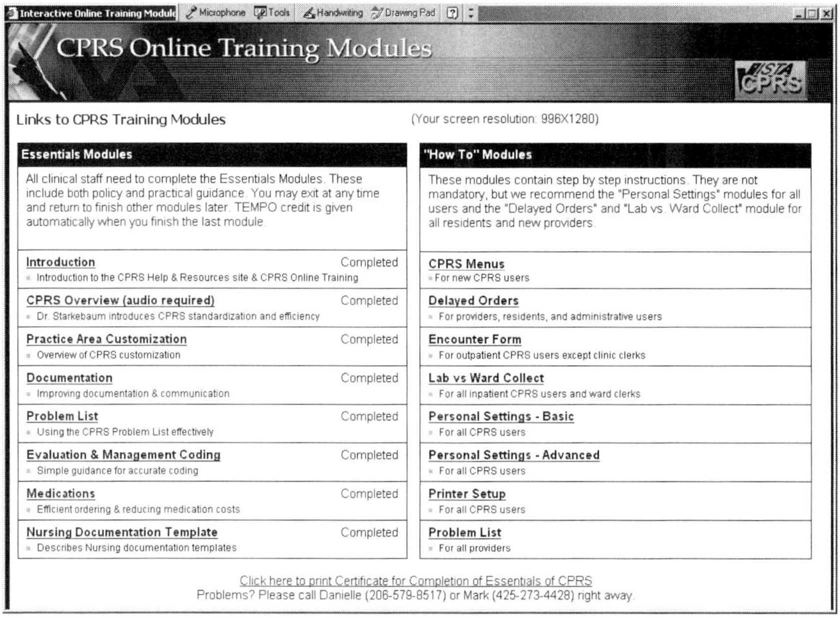

FIGURE 8.1   Website showing index to CPRS web based training modules which are available both within the VA and externally.

opportunity to receive training on a specific issue of their concern or on a new CPRS feature CACs wish to promote.

One point to remember is that user training offers the clinical information team an additional forum for content and software usability testing that should not be underestimated. Clinician trainees often find specific errors or suggest new layouts that are based on their particular areas of expertise. Finally, the team always confirms user access and complete basic user preference set up as the final element of classroom training so that users are "ready for action" as they leave the classroom.

USER SUPPORT AT IMPLEMENTATION AND BEYOND

The most important message for user support is that most clinicians have NO time and limited patience for slow computers or slow support staff. Clinical care typically requires immediate solutions or acceptable workarounds so that care can proceed while the technology catches up. Adequate hardware must be available and functional. Without compromising security, any way to improve access and decrease the steps to logging onto the EMR including single sign-on across all applications is desirable.

Before any go-live, adequate testing including integration testing using valid use cases will save you abundant grief and good will. During implementation you need both face-to-face support staff and super users who are familiar with the specific clinic environment and workflow. The technical team must find a way to get immediate feedback and implement change, sometimes instantaneously if patient safety is at risk.

At Children's, during the go-live implementations support was provided at all times when work was ongoing for a minimum of 2 weeks. A "command center" approach was used staffed by project managers and technical analysts, while clinical and process analysts were stationed with users. Pre-formatted paper "issues forms" were available to report any problems with structured questions needed to help problem-solve. These were ALL logged into a database (Test Director) for tracking to completion.

Depending on the application and workplace, liaisons were provided to transition off the full-time support and local super users were called upon to act as peer-to-peer educators. Seattle Children's continues to staff a 24/7 one-stop Help Desk. The initial call or e-mail is logged in a database, prioritized, and assigned with backup from our technical analyst production support team. We have available asynchronous user support for additional enhancement requests and any hospital incident reports that MAY be related to our EMR are shared with staff and reviewed for possible new enhancements as part of our ongoing quality monitoring. The front-line Help Desk staff are trained post-implementation on our clinical systems and receive weekly updates from the production support team and clinical liaisons that include a "top 5 issues of the week." They handle a remarkably wide array of problems from clinical systems to basic hardware and network problems. Clinical systems analyst support for high priority items is always available. The on-call production support analyst is paged immediately when issues are escalated and can work directly with users, often "ghosting" them on their clinical workstation to resolve issues and inform users about "how to" questions. "Service level agreements" with clear guidelines on how quickly we expect to respond to our busy user community were established.

Monthly meetings with the super user community are supported. Super users are often asked to assist with testing and reviewing prototypes of new functionality. Any user may submit an enhancement request or suggestion via an online tool located on our intranet located on the same page as our incident reporting.

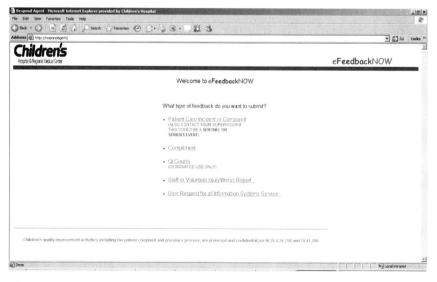

eFeedback for updates and suggestions.

During active CPRS implementation at VA Puget Sound, the CACs of the clinical information team provided on-site coverage 24-hours a day with multiple CACs covering the busiest and most critical units. CACs were issued text pagers, cellular phones, and laptop computers with wireless modems so that they could assist users even when they are between campuses or in other locations. As the implementation progressed, the commitment to on-site coverage between 6:00 am and 7:30 pm during the workweek continued, but coverage during the evening hours and on weekends and holidays was provided by CACs sharing on-call responsibility. The medical center committed to compensating CACs for this continuous coverage with on-call and overtime pay in exchange for this critical service. However, this level of support proved to be quite expensive, both fiscally and in terms of CAC turnover. As the critical mass of CPOE-experienced users was reached, the nature of the calls gradually changed from being CPRS-related to user account or hardware-related, and compensating clinically trained CACs to set up user accounts or repair a troublesome printer was not regarded as an efficient use of CAC skills. In retrospect providing such a high level of clinically trained user support was crucial to our successful implementation, but extending it beyond the initial phases also suppressed the development of a peer support network. As a result of this awareness, the ADPAC, super user, and team assistant programs were upgraded to include user account maintenance and CPRS training, while these more ordinary aspects of user support were transitioned away from CACs.

The Administrative Officer of the Day and Nursing Officer of the Day are staff charged with overseeing the operation of the medical center during non-business hours. They represent VA Puget Sound executive and clinical leadership, critical departments such as the information systems service and biomedical engineering, and important personnel such as ADPACs, who are not on-site 24 hours a day. These staff members also serve as an on-site resource for users experiencing mundane CPRS problems, but frequently page the CAC or network manager on call if needed.

Each CAC in the clinical information management team carries a text pager equipped to receive pages made to multiple numbers. A number appears with each page received, indicating to which pager number the call was made: (1) indicates the page was made to the CACs personal pager number; (2) indicates the page was made to the downtime team; and (3) indicates the page was made to the CAC-on-call pager number. The medical center's network management team also carries these pagers. Members of both teams utilize a web site provided by the paging vendor to broadcast messages to both groups regarding problems with systems status. The use of text pagers capable of receiving pages to multiple numbers as well as messages is vital to supporting users and communication between CAC team members and network managers.

A standard of telephone response to pages within 5 minutes and remote log-in within 10 minutes was established. Requests for assistance that arrive by e-mail are answered within 24 hours. CACs on occasion are required to come to the medical center, for which they are compensated with overtime pay. Information systems staff (programmers and network managers) are likewise on a compensated on-call schedule for issues that cannot be resolved by the on-call CAC. CAC pages are documented in a database for aggregated analysis to provide data for future training initiatives.

Daily CAC rounds, when possible, provides users the opportunity to convey suggestions and complaints, and obtain on-the-spot training for specific issues, without users having to initiate contact. Users can "save their questions" knowing they'll have a daily opportunity to ask them when the CAC appears in their area. During active implementation, twice daily rounds or rounds made every shift were an excellent method for "connecting" with staff, anticipating and resolving problems, provide training, and exhibiting empathy with staff. Post-implementation, it is difficult for an information management team to maintain daily rounds for a large organization, but the technique is still useful on a smaller scale, such as on specific wards or outpatient clinics, or for the first 2 weeks of each resident rotation. Responsive, empathetic contact via daily rounds is usually returned with greater staff enthusiasm and cooperation for new informatics initiatives and mandates.

We recognized it is important to support not only the providers and nurses in the direct patient care locations, but also the pharmacists, dietitians, and staff in the laboratory, radiology, prosthetics, and medical records departments, whose workflow also changed dramatically with the advent of the electronic record. A liaison with each of these departments is crucial to establish (usually the department ADPAC—see below for a more detailed description), and CAC visits to their work areas when possible is much appreciated.

During the phased implementation of CPRS, super users were nominated by their service lines representing all shifts who would serve as a peer resource for CPRS-related issues. Similar to CACs, super users combined clinical skills, technical expertise, and a willingness to help. Post-implementation, super users self-nominate themselves for the role, with supervisory approval, primarily out of personal interest and to receive training from CACs and increased computer access to advanced tools. At some VA facilities, super users are members of the staff education department and as such are eligible for promotion. Tangible compensation for super users' efforts such as bonuses, time off, a recognition luncheon, etc. is well worth the support these users can offer to the day-to-day operations of the medical center. Their continual support raises the overall competence of their immediate co-workers' computer skills, and they are instrumental as new staff and new programs arrive.

In some of the clinical services, team assistants have long served as administrative support for the inpatient house staff teams, sharing their offices, joining in rounds, helping to facilitate consults and discharges. With the introduction of CPRS, these assistants were recognized to be an important complement for user support and training.

Automated Data Processing Application Coordinators (ADPACs) were another important user support resource during CPRS implementation. ADPACs are staff members of their respective services, including clinical bed services such as Medicine, Surgery, Mental Health, Rehab Medicine, and Spinal Cord Injury; clinical order receiving services such as Pharmacy, Laboratory, Radiology, Nursing, and Dietetics; and administrative support services such as enrollment, appointment scheduling, admissions, and billing. ADPAC's serve as the liaison between their department's users and the medical center's information systems department. They are charged with maintenance of their users' computer accounts, training, file maintenance (for large packages such as Pharmacy or Laboratory), patch testing for their respective Vista packages, and report generation. Depending on the size and complexity of the department they serve, they may be full time ADPAC's or perform ADPAC duties in addition to other work. VA Puget Sound instituted a formal ADPAC training course, consisting of different levels of expertise:

   100 Level: Basic ADPAC Skills (Account Maintenance)
   200 Level: Intermediate ADPAC Skills (CPRS Skills, other clinical package skills)
   300 Level: Advanced ADPAC Skills (Advanced CPRS Skills, advanced report generation)

The super user, ADPAC, and team assistant training programs were effective methods of transitioning some of the mundane aspects of user support from CACs to the users' peers or departments. They also represent a professional development ladder for staff interested in

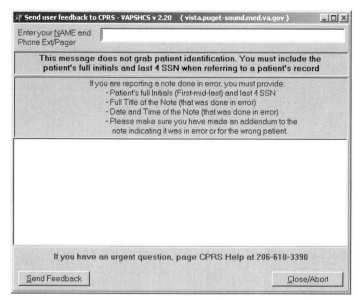

FIGURE 8.2   This small application is easily accessible from CPRS. It permits users to quickly send feedback to, and request non-urgent assistance from, the CPRS support staff.

careers in clinical computing, and ensure a steady resource for CAC succession planning.

Automated mechanisms to support users are also employed. In addition to WBT modules and printable pocket guides, an e-mail link within CPRS was established by which users could send suggestions, complaints, and less-urgent requests for assistance (Figure 8.2). A common request received by this mechanism is for retraction of a progress note entered for the wrong patient. One CAC and the staff of the Health Information Management department (medical records) were designated to monitor and address these messages once a day.

VA Puget Sound employs a Help Desk Monday through Friday 7:30 am–4:30 pm which primarily resolves hardware problems and network account issues. Other VA facilities utilize a regional Help Desk, staffed 24 hours a day, 7 days a week, whose responsibilities are broader.

ONGOING QUALITY IMPROVEMENT AND PATIENT SAFETY INITIATIVES

There are few medical institutions that are NOT using some type of process improvement technique to improve the quality of health-care delivery and reduce both waste and cost in the process of care delivery. At Seattle Children's, we use the Toyota way, lean methodology with ongoing, multidisciplinary process improvement workshops. Staff is freed from their other clinical and administrative duties for up to 1 week of appropriately scoped process improvement projects. These workshops are facilitated by staff skilled in CPI techniques and the project sponsors enlist a Management Guidance Team of administrators and supervisors to review and support the workshop outcomes. Many of these projects now include either direct EMR enhancements or more general institutional information systems support.

It is prudent to anticipate the demand for data that computerization of patient records will create, design interconnected systems that encourage its collection in ways that are transparent to front-line users, and allocate personnel and resources to retrieve, analyze, and report trends to clinical leadership. Individual and aggregated data on medication use, laboratory results, admission and readmission rates, infection rates, ordering patterns, and clinician response to clinical warnings are just a few examples of such information needs. In a "rapid learning" environment, systems should be in place to make use of data analysis to drive quality improvement and patient safety.

DOWNTIME CONTINGENCIES AND RETURN TO ELECTRONIC SYSTEMS

The funny thing is that before you implement your EMR, no one wants to use the computer but once you've been up and running for a few months, and users become "majority adopters," incorporating the new technology into their workflow, then any downtime seems disastrous. Historically physicians complained whenever the paper chart could not be located or delivered in a timely fashion BEFORE an appointment but if the computer system is unavailable, they may become violent.

Automated backups with appropriate downtime reporting to maintain clinical workflow is essential. At Children's, "ops" jobs are scheduled that update downtime reports every 4 hours. These are pushed via FTP files to local workstation hard drives at unit coordination desks that can be accessed and printed from the local workstation even in the event of a complete network failure. The medical center is moving forward with a read-only backup database that was created as part of its disaster recovery planning but meets a strong need to "keep the organization running" even when the EMR is otherwise unavailable. Communicating to users the schedule for anticipated downtimes is essential and scheduled downtime is performed in the early hours of the day to minimize the impact on clinicians. At Children's, the Saturday night nursing staff has become quite adept at managing our monthly planned 4–6-hour downtimes for system upgrades.

Policies and procedures were established. Downtime kits were created including paper order and requisition forms. A downtime report was created that extracted the order set catalog and printed paper order sets that could be used in addition to the standard plain lined order sheet. For "uptimes," we found it imperative to update the EMR particularly to support medication reconciliation. The longer the downtime, the more difficult the task since some of the medications may have been ordered and administered by staff that has gone home. Part of the shift hand-off practice now includes review of med administration during downtime and a process by which the subsequent staff can document administration on behalf of another user based on review of the downtime paper MAR record. We also employ clinical information system analysts to go and assist other clinician users with order entry once the system has recovered.

At VA Puget Sound, the computer system fortunately rarely fails. Staff came to rely on the system so much that published manual procedures to be enacted during a system failure were not familiar; pre-implementation staff forgot manual procedures and staff hired post-implementation were never trained on these procedures. To address this lack of knowledge, a monthly, 4-hour, pre-scheduled, publicized downtime occurs which serves to:

1. Provide time for regular maintenance to be performed which would prevent future unscheduled system failures.
2. Provide a period for clinical staff to practice manual procedures so that they would be familiar in the event of an unscheduled system failure.

This system has proven to be a successful method of significantly reducing the confusion and potential for medical errors resulting from unscheduled downtimes.

Since VA Puget Sound discontinued printing back-up copies of electronic orders and results, accessing patients' records during computer downtime to continue providing patient care is a challenge. For inpatients and outpatients with scheduled appointments, a "health summary" was developed, retrieving active orders, a few days' worth of laboratory, imaging, procedure results, and progress notes, and a medication administration history with space to manually document medication administration during downtime. While the information system is online and functioning, this health summary is collected every six hours for every inpatient and electronically "pushed" from the servers to the C: drives on designated PC's on each ward which are attached to dedicated printers and plugged into outlets with back-up power. In the event of an unexpected downtime, as long as the medical center still has back-up power, the ward staff need only open the password-protected file on the C: drive to view and print the health summaries, which are at most only six hours out of date. For outpatients without scheduled appointments, such as those who might come to the emergency department, VA Puget Sound users can often access VistaWeb during downtime, a web interface to the national VA Health Data Repository, which contains records for millions of veterans. Such access depends on certain components of the network being functional, and is therefore not 100% available.

Ideally, the computer network should never be unavailable and to this end, VA Puget Sound is part of a west coast network, in which a copy of each VA medical center's database is maintained. Information is continually exchanged between the systems and in the event one fails, the network is capable of supplying information to the "down" medical center, making the downtime essentially transparent to the staff. When the failed system again becomes available, it synchronizes its database with the network as before the system failure.

Concurrently with these back-up mechanisms, it is crucial to have clear, concise downtime policies and procedures available to staff on paper in their work area, along with the manual forms they will need to operate. It is critical that departments review and produce the procedures and forms together, so the non-computerized flow of orders, results, and documentation is coordinated. In large, networked organizations such as the VA, seamless, timely communication between local, regional, and national network managers, between network managers and support staff such as CACs, and between CACs and the user community is also critical, and merits policies that outline specific procedures, roles, responsibilities, and service level agreements. At VA Puget Sound, every downtime episode is analyzed and debriefed, and lessons learned are incorporated into established procedures.

NEW CHALLENGES AND LESSONS LEARNED

The sheer number of clinical alerts, reminders, and pop-ups has exploded to the point that they detract from clinical care, even when they are timely and appropriate. The typical response from users is to simply "tune out ALL alerts" which negatively impacts patient safety. At Seattle Children's we are now embarking on a regular and formal review of our alert and reminder warnings, particularly those related to our custom created dose range checking. We look to see how many alerts/reminder will pop up in given timeframe and analyze the number and reason of alert overrides. Based on this data, we hope to improve the efficiency, appropriateness, and timeliness of our alerts to avoid ongoing fatigue. We are always soliciting feedback from users about alerts that they see as fundamentally and clinically "wrong."

Encounter selection: In most CPOE systems, orders are related to clinical encounters or visits and these may be designed more by business services than clinicians. In our ambulatory environment where a single patient may visit multiple clinics and providers during a single day or week, we may have difficulty identifying the correct clinical encounter. Clinicians are more concerned about "getting their orders correct" so we have provided several approaches to minimize the need to become an expert in billing services in order to provide clinical care. Whenever possible, clinicians work from location or provider worklists and we expect the clinical system to attach the appropriate clinical encounter. Our greatest problems occur between ambulatory visits or in preparation for scheduled inpatient care. In clinical areas where this is common, we have identified scheduling and admitting services contact to help the clinicians select the correct encounter from the start.

Information overload in documentation: This refers to the volume of information in progress notes. At VA Puget Sound, this in part was due to the ubiquitous use of "patient data objects," a popular feature in CPRS by which patient-related results can be automatically imported into progress notes. Another factor was the ability in CPRS for staff to create note templates for their personal use. Yet another factor was the differing uses of progress notes: documentation with the intent to communicate with other providers, documentation with the intent to organize record review, and documentation with the intent to meet regulatory requirements. In 2005, VA Puget Sound instituted a standardized note template format which meets these three note-writing intents while allowing a high degree of customization according to users' personal and departmental preferences. It introduced a horizontal line to the note format, above which the author succinctly writes his/her synthesis and analysis of the patient's record, and below which the supporting information, whether imported automatically as "patient data objects," copied and pasted from elsewhere in the patient's chart, or entered manually by the author, would be captured.

Copy/Paste: The ability to copy and paste text using the Windows clipboard has introduced ethical, legal, and patient safety concerns. It contributes to the volume of text that needs to be waded through in order to get to the crux of the note. Proper attribution may not be given. It can contribute to undetected errors by copying text from the wrong patient's record or copying and pasting events out of sequence. A policy outlining the use of copy/paste functionality should be established at minimum, and a monitoring system, either manual or electronic, should be employed. In future iterations of CPRS, copied text will appear in a different color and font in electronic documents.

Anticipate use of structured data: VA Puget Sound incorporates structured data into notes and orders rather than simply capturing narrative free-text. Structured data can be captured, aggregated, analyzed, researched, and returned to the health-care system in the form of guidelines and other modes of decision support in a continuous improvement feedback loop, A key advancement toward this effort was the development and release of the Clinical Reminder package, which provides a mechanism for "health factors" to be captured as progress notes are entered. These health factors can be aggregated, analyzed, and employed in clinical reminder logic to drive clinical guidelines and other mechanisms for decision support. On the ordering side, "orderable items" serve the same function as health factors, namely, discrete, structured data elements which serve dual purposes: to get "something" ordered or documented, and to capture that "something" in such a way that logic can be applied to it to drive decision support and that it can be captured for analysis and research. The challenge we face in capturing the structured data we anticipate needing is that our clinicians must use templated progress notes and orders, rather than interacting with the medical record in the free form manner to which they expect. It is not natural to place orders or compose a progress note by clicking on a series of checkboxes. A natural language interface that allows clinicians to freely type orders and notes into the medical record while CPRS simultaneously references, matches, and captures health factors and orderable items would launch CPRS from the realm of an electronic replacement for the paper medical record to a powerful tool for patient safety, decision support, research, and health-care policy. Fortunately, VA developers are investigating such an interface.

Retraction issues: One caveat to the potential increase in structured data capture through entry of progress notes and orders are the ramifications if a note or order was entered for the wrong patient. VA Puget Sound has a procedure for clinical staff to request the retraction of erroneous note text; however, no mechanism exists for retraction of embedded data elements or orders. This could be disastrous if not addressed: if a health factor documenting a colonoscopy is entered erroneously through a progress note, and the note is retracted but the health factor is not, the computerized reminder to perform a colonoscopy may be erroneously turned off for the wrong patient. In the worse case scenario, the patient would miss a crucial screening procedure that would have detected the presence of colon cancer. Fortunately, we are developing a new version of the feature described in Figure 8.2, which will identify data elements which were entered within an erroneously entered note, and ask the sender which should be retracted.

Human factors engineering: Humans interact with technology and sometimes produce results that were not expected by the technology designers; with CPOE such interactions can produce errors that contribute to patient morbidity and mortality. Implementation of EMR systems often reveal startlingly erroneous assumptions made by programmers and users, and CPOE designers must be alert to the possibility of the system itself, or how it is configured, contributing to medical errors. Patient safety must be paramount to the clinical information management team, medical center leadership, programmers, network managers, and designers of the EMR. Developers and commercial software vendors must be willing to respond quickly to resolve cognitive engineering problems. To illustrate this we offer three examples:

1. In 2004, JCAHO published a list of unsafe abbreviations which were required to be eliminated from the medical vocabulary and a list which were recommended for elimination. "QD" appeared on the recommended list, with the suggestion that "Daily" be substituted. Many VA facilities followed the recommendation and changed "QD" to "Daily" in their medication schedule files referenced by CPRS. However, clinicians persisted in entering "QD." Since "QD" was no longer on file, CPRS, following the strict computational standards of the computing world which do not take human interpretation into consideration, offered the closest match on file: "Q12H." Fortunately, this example of cognitive engineering was discovered in a test environment and fixed before the patch was released.

2. In early versions of CPRS, the medication selection screen employed an AutoComplete feature also popular in Microsoft Word, which allowed clinicians to enter a few characters of a lengthy drug name for which they may not have known the correct spelling and CPRS would complete the entry. However, the auto-completed entry offered by CPRS may not have been the drug intended by the clinician. A clinician could desire to order "Procardia," a calcium-channel blocker, and enter "Procar," not realizing that the closest match to his/her

entry is "Procarbazine," an antineoplastic agent, since the "b" in Procarbazine comes before the "d" in Procardia. Fortunately, the AutoComplete feature was promptly disabled.

3. An important feature of CPRS is the ability to document patients' use of over-the-counter medications, herbal products, and non-VA legend prescriptions. In the effort to introduce an intuitive interface for this purpose, the screen for entering this "Non-VA" documentation was designed to appear similar to the prescription ordering screen. In fact, the "Non-VA" screen was familiar enough that clinicians used it to order prescriptions, not realizing that it was for documentation only, and their patients failed to receive the medication. Fortunately, this was recognized and is promptly being addressed through redesign of the dialog.

Medication reconciliation: This process is complex and challenging, even the setting of a comprehensive, well-designed, user friendly EMR. Patients are often unaware of many of the details about their medications or uncomfortable sharing information about complementary therapies. It is still rare for patients to present to the hospital with an up to date, complete listing of their medications and allergy history, or even all of their medications in a plastic bag. At Seattle Children's, pediatric weight-based dosing makes prescription writing and medication reconciliation even more challenging since few systems effectively allow for the input and output of prescribing information that includes understandable dosing in both milligram and volume amounts. You may understand that you want to deliver 250 milligrams but the patient's family members must understand that that's one teaspoon or 5 ml on their dosing syringe. In fact, in pediatrics, errors in medication administration are frequent and few commercially available EMR formularies offer all of the functionality required for efficient and safe pediatric prescribing.

CONCLUSION

Much has been published regarding EMR implementations and the planning, resources, institutional support, and tremendous effort they require in order to be successful. However, to sustain an EMR long term after the excitement (and short-term funding) of implementation has died down and realize the benefits computerized records can provide to quality improvement, workflow, patient safety, cost reduction, and public health, is equally if not more important. A prudent organization will recognize and plan for this even as it makes implementation plans.

REFERENCES

[1] Ash JS et al. Principles for a successful computerized physician order entry implementation. AMIA Annual Symposium Proc. 2003; 36–40.
[2] Ammenwerth E, Talmon J, Ash JS, et al. Impact of CPOE on mortality rates – contradictory findings, important messages. Methods Inf Med. 2006; 45: 586–93.

PART

III

REGULATORY, LEGAL, AND ORGANIZATIONAL ISSUES

9

HEALTH INFORMATION MANAGEMENT AND THE EMR

JACQUIE ZEHNER

Patient Data Services, Harborview Medical Center, Seattle, WA

USES OF THE ELECTRONIC MEDICAL RECORD (EMR)

The electronic medical record (EMR) allows clinical information to be available at the point of care.

One important advantage of the EMR is that it allows multiple accesses concurrently. While a patient is hospitalized, it has been estimated an average of 100 care providers will access the patient's record. Many medical center employees outside the immediate care team will also need access to the patient's information, including clinical researchers, employees from radiology, laboratory, pathology, physical therapy, occupational therapy, pharmacy, quality improvement, infection control, health information management, compliance, information technology, utilization management, risk management, and revenue cycle management.

The medical center must define it's legal medical record and determine what belongs in the medical record and what doesn't.

GOALS OF HEALTH INFORMATION MANAGEMENT WITHIN THE MEDICAL CENTERS

The goal for health-care providers is ease of access to locate clinical information needed to monitor and make patient care decisions. This is no easy task. Health-care delivery is complicated with many professionals serving numerous roles. There are countless pieces of data collected and recorded on a patient. The goal for the author documenting the record is to determine what is important and to create a clear, legible note as briefly as possible. Other health-care providers do not want to sift through lengthy reports to find key pieces of information.

The organization and layout of individual notes and the entire medical record is a challenge as well and the countless documents that make up a complicated patients' record is impressive.

TYPICAL CATEGORIES OR SECTIONS OF A MEDICAL RECORD

Registration and Admission Information;
History and Physical Examination;
Physician Progress Notes;
Physician Consultations and Referral Information;
Physician Orders;
Nursing Records;
Flowsheets—Fluid Input and Output, Vital Signs;
Infusion Records;
Immunization/Skin Testing;
Ancillary Service Records—Social Work, Physical Therapy, Rehab Therapy, Occupational Therapy, etc.;
Medication Records—Medication Profile, Medication Administration Record;
Surgical Reports—Anesthesia, Operating Room and Surgical Procedure Reports, Pre-Operative and Postoperative Care Notes;
Radiology Report and Images;
Laboratory Results;
Pathology Reports;
Other Diagnostics Reports;
Emergency Room Records;
Obstetrics and Birth Records;
Seclusion and Restraint Records;
Discharge Information;
Patient Alerts;
Problem List;
Pre-Hospital Documentation—Ambulance and Life Flight Records, Skilled Nursing Facility Transfer Record;

Patient Education;
Patient Authorization and Consents; and
Insurance and Financial Information.

Within each category listed above there will be multiple form names and associated documents. It's not uncommon that a medical center will have hundreds if not thousands of document names that fall within the categories.

Also considered part of a legal medical record are other media such as imaging films, photographs, video, and audio recordings.

Because there are numerous numbers of professionals providing care to the patient, across many departments and different shifts, the medical record serves as a primary communication tool for patient care. The EMR is a safety tool and it can hinder patient safety if something is recorded in error, not reported promptly, illegible, or inaccessible. So timely, legible, complete, and concise documentation with ease of access is highly important to quality patient care and the goal of the EMR.

In a teaching medical center, where residents, medical students, and fellows provide patient care and document in the medical record, it is important they follow good documentation practices, including legibly identifying their self, role, and credentials. Once an individual completes their rotation, it can be nearly impossible retrospectively to identify the author of a note. Prior to completing the residency or fellowship, all documentation is to be completed. To leave a program without having met the documentation and record keeping requirements is a serious offense and will leave the chief of service, the medical director, and medical record committee with the burden to either piece together the documentation or close the incomplete record.

HYBRID OF MEDICAL RECORD MEDIA

HOW INFORMATION IS ENTERED INTO THE ELECTRONIC MEDICAL RECORD (EMR)

There are basically three main mechanisms to get information into an EMR. They are: Direct entry, electronic interfaces, and document imaging (scanning). The first method of direct entry occurs when the health-care provider accesses the EMR application, opens a template designated for input and enters the documentation, electronically signs, and saves the information. Examples of applications for direct entry can be CPOE, physician progress or clinic notes, Nursing inpatient vital signs and progress notes, and other ancillary services as well. Most medical centers use a number of different electronic application systems that are separated from the core EMR. Because of this, electronic interfaces are built to move data from the host system to the EMR. Common examples of applications interfaced are radiology, laboratory, transcription, pharmacy, and many diagnostic systems. Building and managing interfaces can be labor intensive and expensive. This may be cause for medical centers to choose a vendor with many application products to allow for an integrated approach and minimize the number of interfaces. The third mechanism is document imaging. When medical record documentation is on paper, it can be scanned and viewed in the EMR.

Most medical centers have a blend for how information gets into the EMR; because of this, many continue to rely on paper to a great extent.

At many medical centers there are several locations and systems; providers and those requiring access must locate the clinical information they seek. A typical scenario for an inpatient facility early in their EMR implementation may look something like this: Nursing documentation in system A; laboratory, radiology, and transcribed reports in system B; and a paper medical record on the unit which includes handwritten orders, physician and ancillary progress notes, emergency records, and other documents.

A medical center with a more sophisticated EMR will have a number of direct entry applications within their EMR and may look like this:

  PACS imaging, EKG readings, CPOE, Physician documentation direct entry templated progress notes, Nursing templated documentation and flow sheet, Pharmacy medication management application, Medication Administration Records (MAR), Emergency Room documentation;

  Interfaced transcribed documents such as surgical, consultation, and discharge summary reports; radiology, laboratory, pathology, and other diagnostic test reports; and

  Scanned operating room pre- and post-surgical and anesthesia records, pre-hospital records, authorization, and consents.

THE TRANSITION TO THE EMR TAKES YEARS

During this transition period, it can be quite challenging for medical record users, new to the system, to know where to find documentation. Most medical centers will create a medical record roadmap telling users which system to go to, i.e., paper or electronic. Once in the system where the information belongs, the user needs knowledge to navigate the system to find where the information is located. The systems are designed with the goal to be logical in their layout, but the volume and multitude of information and the complexity of patient care means layers of categories and sections for specific information to reside. The user learns to navigate the system to quickly find the information needed when monitoring and caring for the patient.

Besides the medical record created and maintained for the care and safety of the patient, there are other uses of the medical record. They include continuity of patient care, regulatory and compliance oversight, insurance and payer requirements, clinical research and public health reporting, professional and organizational perform-ance improvement, and legal purposes.

HEALTH INFORMATION MANAGEMENT

The Health Information Management (HIM) Department[1] is made up of a number of components. These include but are not limited to Coding, Medical Transcription, Medical Record Analysis and Com-pletion Monitoring, Document Imaging, Master Patient Index Man-agement, Release of Information, HIM Education and Training, and Documentation Abstracting and Audits. Following is a general description of several areas.

CODING CLASSIFICATION AND PAYMENT SYSTEM

HIM Coders are employees with a great degree of training and educa-tion in coding classification systems and rule application. They are generally certified specifically in coding or come with years of experience.

Medical facilities and physician services use ICD-9-CM and CPT4 codes to describe diagnoses treated and services delivered; however, each falls under a different payment system for how the codes equate to payment. Additionally, there are different coding guidelines within a medical facility when a patient receives inpatient versus outpatient care. Coding is complicated; however, it is extremely important. Health-care providers pay great attention to coding services as it

[1] In some medical centers Health Information Management may be known as Medical Records, Patient Data Services, or by another name.

directly impacts revenue, organizational ranking in comparison with peer institutions, and public health reporting.

Codes are assigned to diagnoses and procedures found within the medical record. These codes summarize the clinical care and treatment of the patient. Coding is the use of numeric and alphanumeric codes as a way to describe the clinical information. Diagnosis coding systems are used to report the reason the patient received health-care services. In the case of accidents, diagnosis codes may also be used to report how and where the accident occurred. A procedure coding system is used to describe what services or items the patient received. Reimbursement and statistical reporting in healthcare are based on the codes. There are many rules to follow in assigning codes within the classification system. These codes are very important as they determine how physicians and medical facilities will receive revenue for services. For example, if a patient is admitted with the diagnosis of dyspnea and found to have both pneumonia and respiratory failure, adding these additional codes may affect revenue received. These codes are also used for reporting and benchmarking for health-care statistics.

ICD-9-CM is the primary coding system used for reimbursement for inpatient hospital services. It stands for "International Classification of Diseases, 9th Revision, Clinical Modifications." ICD-9-CM is a modified version of the World Health Organization's (WHO) ICD-9 Coding System. The term "Clinical Modifications" were made to enhance ICD-9 for uses other than statistical tracking. The Public Health Service and the Centers for Medicare and Medicaid Services (CMS) have published "Official ICD-9-CM Guidelines" which are available from the NCHS web site.

ICD-9-CM contains both diagnosis and procedure codes. Medical facilities use both ICD-9-CM diagnosis and procedure codes for inpatient stays, and only diagnosis codes used to record outpatient diagnosis. The classification system termed Current Procedural Terminology (CPT-4) is the other primary coding classification system widely used. CPT-4 is used to identify procedures and ancillary charges.

In 1993, WHO published ICD-10 which has been adopted by several countries. The United States plans to move to this in the future. ICD-9-CM contains thousands of codes. ICD-10 has more codes (5500 more than ICD-9) to allow even more specific reporting of diseases.

HCPCS stands for "Healthcare Common Procedure Coding System." HCPCS is a procedure coding system used for reporting services, supplies, and equipment. There are two levels of HCPCS codes.

HCPCS Level 1 is the CPT coding system as developed and maintained by the American Medical Association. As mentioned earlier, CPT-4 is used primarily to report practitioner services and technical/facility component services provided in conjunction with practitioner services.

HCPCS level II are national procedure codes generally used to supplement level 1 (CPT).

When working within the inpatient medical center you will hear the terms ICD-9 and Diagnostic Related Groups (DRG) in correlation to coding and billing. ICD-9-CM codes are the basis for determining the DRG, by which the inpatient medical center is paid.

DRGs come under the Centers for Medicare/Medicaid Services (CMS) Inpatient Prospective Payment System (IPPS). Under IPPS, hospitals receive a prospectively determined fixed payment amount for most inpatient cases, regardless of the costs incurred by the hospital to treat the patient. DRGs went into effect in the early 1980s as an incentive for hospitals to operate efficiently and minimize unnecessary cost. IPPS does not apply to the following types of inpatient acute care facilities: psychiatric, rehabilitation, children's long-term care, and cancer hospitals. Most payers use DRGs to reimburse inpatient hospital claims.

In the outpatient medical center facility setting, the Balanced Budget Act of 1997 provides authority for Centers for Medicare/Medicaid Services (CMS) to implement the Outpatient Prospective Payment System (OPPS). OPPS is based on APC, which stands for Ambulatory Payment Classifications. APCs are groupings that are derived from CPT-4 procedure codes. Services in each APC are similar clinically and in terms of the resources they require. Reimbursement is based on the APC for the medical facility. APCs went into effect in April 2000.

Physicians are reimbursed differently than medical center facilities. They are not reimbursed based on DRGs or APCs, but rather resource-based relative value units (RBRVUs). They are more commonly referred to as relative value units (RVUs), which are based on CPT-4 procedure codes. Additionally, RVUs quantify the relative work, practice expense, and malpractice costs for specific physician services to establish payment. This system was established in the early 1990s and is the prevailing model.

Pay for Performance is a newer system and payment methodology which may impact the current RVU model. Patients commonly receive two bills: one from the physician, and one from the facility.

HIM DICTATION AND TRANSCRIPTION SERVICES

Medical Centers typically have physicians talk into a digital recording device the following medical record reports: History and Physical Examinations, Operative Reports, Consultations, and Discharge Summaries. While all documentation in a medical record are considered essential to the patient's clinical care, these four in particular are important enough to warrant expensive transcription services in many medical centers. Transcription of these reports allows for legible formatted concise reports.

HIM medical transcriptionists are also known as medical language specialists. They are trained to listen to digital recorded voices and transcribe them using correct medical terminology and English grammar use. This can be quite challenging given the numerous specialty areas, new medical terms, medications, and surgical equipment. Some physicians can speak quickly, with poor enunciation, and in noisy environments. Any of these can create challenges for a medical transcriptionist. Transcription service turnaround of reports generally takes 24–48 hours from dictation to transcription. Many physicians now directly enter their reports into the EMR and skip the dictation step or use voice recognition software to convert their spoken words into text.

This allows for immediate availability of their documentation.

MEDICAL RECORD ANALYSIS AND COMPLETION MONITORING

Regulatory bodies such as Medicare (CMS), state Division of Health, and national accreditation organizations, such as the Joint Commission, establish standards for medical record completion. There are many standards established. It's inherent that each medical center outlines their standards within Medical Center policy and Medical Staff Bylaws, Rules, and Regulations. These policy, bylaws, rules, and regulations are to fall within the parameters of state law and the accrediting organizations they subscribe to.

The HIM department supports the medical center and physicians by monitoring medical record completion and providing medical center leaders and the medical director with reports. This allows medical center leadership to work with employees and physicians to improve and comply with quality and timely medical record documentation.

Medical Centers are highly regulated and are often visited by surveyors who review medical records to learn of the quality care delivered and identify any deficits of rules and regulations. Medical

Centers can be cited when deficits are noted in medical record documentation and worse they can loose their certifications and licenses to practice healthcare based on poor medical record documentation. It behooves medical center leadership to invest in tools, such as an EMR, that can promote health-care communications, patient safety, and regulatory standards. The HIM department supports this cause by providing the monitoring and the feedback to leadership.

DOCUMENT IMAGING

Document scanning is the process of converting a paper document into an electronic image and having it available within the EMR. Because there is a medical record structure with categories, the scanned images have to be mapped to specific category locations. This assists users to locate information within the record. The process of mapping can occur through a systematized form process where each form contains a bar code system, which performs this function. There is generally a second bar code label attached to a completed patient form, which identifies the patient and date of service. There are generally several steps to the scanning process. First the records have to be prepared to assure a good image, followed by scanning, reviewing for a quality image, and then releasing into the EMR for viewing. An important step in scanning documents is to index them in a useful fashion. Finding the document needed within a large collection of scanned documents is far easier for clinicians if the name assigned to the scanned document is clear and descriptive. Some EMR document scanning projects are less useful because of weaknesses in the indexing process.

DATABASE MANAGEMENT: MASTER PATIENT INDEX (MPI) MANAGEMENT AND PROVIDER REFERRAL DATABASES

While the HIM department is not generally database engineers, they are often responsible for managing the database for quality and accuracy and resolving discrepancies.

MPI

Each medical center should have one and only one unique medical record number for each patient. There are many reasons why one medical record number can be assigned to more than one person and reasons why two or more medical record numbers can be assigned to one person. The job of the MPI area is to proactively identify and resolve these types of scenarios. Should two persons' clinical information be placed in one record, it is their job to work with clinicians to separate it out into two individually identifiable numbers and records. When a patient ends up with several medical record numbers, this generally means he/she has more than one medical record; it is this area's responsibility to merge them into one record and one medical record number. This is an important patient safety requirement. These types of scenarios can occur when a patient enters the hospital in an unconscious state and with no identification, or similar names, there are other scenarios as well. Unfortunately this is quite common.

Provider Database

The quality and accuracy of physician names and addresses is critical to assure that referring physicians receive patient care information for monitoring and following the progress of their patient's. There are many physicians with same or similar names. To send patient inform-ation to the wrong physician or address can result in a HIPAA privacy violation. And more importantly, critical health information may be not reach the continuing care provider in a timely way. Rules are established to manage databases to minimalize errors.

RELEASE OF INFORMATION

There are a number of reasons for patients to request their medical records be released to another organization. Examples include to support disability and life insurance underwriting policy, other health-care providers for continuing health-care services, attorneys for various lawsuit and claims work, Labor and Industry claims, to name a few. HIPAA federal regulations, as well as other federal rules, and state laws govern how covered entities, such as medical centers, must manage the release of protected patient health information.

HIM release of information employees are specifically trained to assure all regulations are followed to make sure the patient's right to disclosure or limitation of disclosure is followed.

Additionally, medical records can be subpoenaed with 14-day notice, and court ordered as well. HIM release of information employees are trained to prepare and follow applicable rules for proper preparation and disclosure.

Oversight agencies such as Public Health for Reporting and Division of Health for Survey have access to patient information without authorization for disclosure.

HIM CREDENTIALS AND CERTIFICATIONS

There are several credentials and a number of certifications that HIM employees typically hold.

They are:

Health Information Management

- Registered Health Information Administrator (RHIA); and
- Registered Health Information Technician (RHIT).

Coding

- Certified Coding Associate (CCA);
- Certified Coding Specialist (CCS);
- Certified Coding Specialist-Physician-based (CCS-P); and
- Certified Professional Coder (CPC).

Healthcare Privacy and Security

- Certified in Healthcare Privacy (CHP);
- Certified in Healthcare Privacy and Security (CHPS); and
- Certified in Healthcare Security (CHS).

10

LEGAL ISSUES IN MEDICAL RECORDS/HEALTH INFORMATION MANAGEMENT

SALLY BEAHAN

Patient Data Services, University of Washington Medical Center, Seattle, WA

Use and content of the medical record, whether in paper or electronic form, is governed by a variety of groups and regulations, some of which vary between organizations. As clinical computing systems are installed and maintained, this oversight continues and needs to be understood and considered when changes in health information are proposed.

ORGANIZATIONAL GROUPS AND REGULATIONS THAT AFFECT MEDICAL RECORDS

MEDICAL STAFF BYLAWS, POLICY & PROCEDURES

All hospitals are required by law to maintain bylaws that govern the medical staff in addition to specific policies and procedures that guide medical staff decision making and processes. The Medical Staff Policy & Procedure manual should contain a specific chapter on medical records. The purpose of this chapter is to outline required elements within the medical record as well as who can document, when co-signatures are required, and define the guidelines around timeliness of the documentation.

At UW and other organizations, the Medical Director's office over-sees the Medical Staff Policies & Procedures and it is up to the Medical Director or a designee to update these documents. If changes are needed to Policies & Procedures governing the medical record, a recommenda-tion would typically come from the Medical Record Committee. The Medical Staff Bylaws would not be expected to change very often because the change process is more complicated, whereas one may expect the Policies & Procedures to change more regularly as regulatory requirements change or new policies are adopted. An example of a change that may be made to the medical record portion of the Policies & Procedures is a change in how long physicians have to sign documents entered in the medical record. Regulatory bodies expect that day-to-day practice conforms with Medical Staff Policies & Procedures.

It is good practice to review the Medical Staff Policies & Proce-dures annually to ensure any recent regulatory changes are reflected.

Specificity in policies can be a double-edged sword. Each depart-ment can have policies that are more rigid than guidelines within the Medical Staff Policies & Procedures. However, the Medical Staff Poli-cies & Procedures must minimally match the standards of the Joint Commission; so there's assurance that you have a mechanism in place to meet their regulatory requirements. For example, consider the med-ical record signature requirements by the Joint Commission, which states that entries (dictated or directly entered) in the medical record be signed by the author within 30 days. Your Medical Staff Policies & Procedures can be even more rigid and state that physicians have 21 days to sign their documents, but a problem arises if you have another policy within the Emergency Room that states you cannot bill facility or professional fee charges without signed medical record documenta-tion. You might want to consider creating a more stringent signature policy in the Emergency Room to facilitate the billing process.

Additionally, it is important to remember that since you are obli-gated to abide by the Medical Staff Policies & Procedures, you should not set policies that are too hard to follow. For example, if an attending physician co-signature is not a regulatory requirement of the Joint Commission, you might want to think twice before having a Medical Staff Policy & Procedure that requires attending physician co-signatures for all admission history and physical documents. Enforcing this requirement may become so difficult for the medical record department that it's not worth having such a detailed require-ment stated within the Policies & Procedures.

MEDICAL RECORD COMMITTEE

The medical record committee provides guidance, makes decisions, and creates policies related to medical record documentation guidelines, timeliness of documentation, the content of the medical record, who should be allowed to document into the record, how records are maintained, and who should have access to the records. In this ever changing electronic world, the medical record committee provides guidance and insight to the organization as to where documentation should be located in the electronic medical record (EMR) and how moving documentation from a paper world to an electronic world should be prioritized from a patient care perspective. Prioritizing what documentation goes into the EMR first is essential to the success of the EMR project. The organization needs the input from direct care providers and the committee to ensure they are making EMR decisions that will support the medical staff. Buy-in from the medical staff is critical and the medical record committee provides the avenue for care providers to give feedback and input so that an EMR which works for them is created. An example of a decision that the medical record committee can help with is defining how many years worth of historical nursing documentation should be available in the EMR. The input from those working directly with patients is essential. The IT department needs this type of input when designing the EMR because they are not providing direct patient care and will not always know which elements of the medical records are essential for patient care. This committee is the link between the medical staff and the medical record department. The committee can make recommendations to the Medical Director's office to update the Medical Staff Policies & Procedures.

The committee is most successful when the majority of the committee members are physicians. Nursing representation is important as well as they have a vested interest in medical record policies and guidelines. Leadership from the medical record department is critical as well as some representation from hospital administration. It is essential to have a strong physician chair this group as he/she may be called upon to get their peers to comply with provisions within the Medical Staff Policies & Procedures.

If the leadership of the medical record department is having difficulty with enforcing the signature guidelines for the medical record, the medical record committee will provide the support to gain compliance among the medical staff. It's their peers telling them what they need to do, so it goes over much better than having a non-physician telling them. Additionally, if the medical record department is thinking about moving the documentation currently in paper to the EMR, this committee serves as the sounding board for ideas and provides input as to what will work and what their preferences are in order to facilitate their day-to-day workflow.

THE MEDICAL RECORD DEPARTMENT

Most hospitals have a separate department or division known variously as Medical Records, Information Management, or Patient Data Services. Beginning in the earliest days of modern medical centers, this department had responsibility for the integrity, availability, and operations of the medical record. That role continues, and in some organizations is combined with or works in conjunction with the team implementing and operating clinical computing systems such as the EMR.

FEDERAL LAWS AND ENTITIES THAT AFFECT MEDICAL RECORDS

HEALTH INFORMATION PORTABILITY AND ACCOUNTABILITY ACT (HIPAA[1])

HIPAA has had an enormous impact on medical center practices and regulations since its enactment. It was approved in 2003 with the expectation for compliance by 2005. The law requires that reasonable controls exists for electronic protected health information (ePHI).

HIPAA encompasses protected health information including but not limited to medical records (both electronic and paper), conversations related to patient information, documentation that includes elements of patient information, i.e., billing documents, admitting reports, and any other sources of patient information including recycled paper that contains patient information. Additional policies and staff training were required in order to ensure the medical record department processes fell within the HIPAA guidelines and expectations.

The privacy and security policies intersect within HIPAA. Their purpose is to ensure the confidentiality, integrity, and availability of

---

[1] A common error is to use the abbreviation HIPPA rather than HIPAA. Avoid this!

all ePHI that a covered entity (such as a medical center) creates, receives, maintains, or transmits. It is the expectation that an organization protects against any reasonably anticipated threats or hazards to the security or integrity of such information in addition to protecting against any reasonably anticipated uses or disclosures of such information that are not permitted or required by law. Compliance by an organization's workforce is also an expectation of the HIPAA laws. Security regulations require administrative safeguards such as a security management process, risk analysis, a sanction policy, as well as an information system activity review. In addition, physical safeguards are required such as facility access controls, workstation use, and workstation security policies. Technical safeguards are also an important component of HIPAA in order to cover access control, audit controls, data integrity, and personal or organizational authentication.

Access to protected health information is governed by state and federal laws. Anyone involved in the treatment, payment, or healthcare operations and has a "need to know" may access the minimal protected health information necessary to satisfy the functions of their job.

CENTERS FOR MEDICARE AND MEDICAID SERVICES (CMS)

CMS is a branch of the federal Department of Health and Human Services. It developed Conditions of Participation and Conditions for Coverage that health-care organizations must meet in order to begin and continue participating in the Medicare and Medicaid programs. These minimum health and safety standards are the foundation for improving quality and protecting the health and safety of beneficiaries as well as providing minimum standards that providers and suppliers must meet in order to be Medicare and Medicaid certified. CMS recognizes hospitals accredited by the Joint Commission as meeting all requirements for Medicare participation. There are specific Conditions of Participation related to medical records which outline the completion, filing, and maintenance of the records. Minimum requirements relating to the retention of the records is outlined as well as the coding, indexing, and the confidentiality requirements for the records. The guidelines set forth by the Conditions of Participation's are similar to but not as detailed as the Joint Commission requirements which are outlined more specifically later in this chapter.

Ensuring that there is adequate and concise documentation for each patient is critical for a number of reasons. Not only does it provide facts, findings, and observations to assist health-care professionals in diagnosing and treating their patients but it also assists with the planning for treatment and the patient's need for potential monitoring over time. Documentation also assists with accurate and timely reimbursement for services provided as payers may require reasonable documentation to support the charges billed for patient visits. More and more payers are implementing rules around what services they will or will not reimburse for. The requirements around documentation for billing are simple—if it's not documented, it didn't happen! A facility should never bill for services that they cannot provide documentation for to prove the services happened. If this happens it is considered billing fraud. In teaching facilities, if a resident documents the services provided into the medical record, the attending physician must at a minimum document their participation and presence during the visit in order to bill for services. CMS has defined specific billing guidelines providers (mostly physicians) must follow to assign Evaluation and Management (E&M) codes used in billing for visits and consultations. The E&M codes are levels of service that relate to reimbursement under the E&M guidelines. The key elements of service that must be documented are history, examination, and medical decision making. Having medical coders check documentation prior to billing or better yet, having an electronic system for documentation and generation of charges by the health-care provider is ideal.

The Office of the Inspector General (OIG) is a division within the Department of Health and Human Services (HHS) and has specific authority to investigate anyone or any institution that has fraudulently submitted claims. The OIG has the ability to seek civil and/or criminal penalties for a variety of reasons. If a facility is audited for charges they billed for and they cannot produce adequate documentation to support the charges, the facility can face serious civil and criminal penalties, large multimillion dollar fines, and possible exclusion from federally funded programs. The OIG posts all cases where fines and penalties have been carried out on their web site which is accessible to the public and can cause an institution or individual provider years of scrutiny.

STATE LAWS THAT AFFECT MEDICAL RECORD DOCUMENTATION

The Washington Department of Health has guidelines at the state level; but none are as stringent as those of the Joint Commission. Hospitals typically follow the Joint Commission guidelines for required elements and timelines for documentation. Other states may have different guidelines and regulations that should be understood by clinical computing system leaders.

Every state has a retention schedule which guides hospitals on how long they are to retain certain types of records. Types of records are differentiated such as medical records, radiology films, pathology slides, incident reports, etc. and each type may have a different timeline for retention. It is important to ensure your facility is aware of and follows the retention guidelines as holding records for longer than is necessary may actually set your facility up for greater risk management issues. This is because records in your possession are deemed as discoverable within the public records query process. If you no longer have the records and are following state guidelines, you don't have records to produce if you do receive a public record request. As electronic records become more and more common, it is important to ensure the retention schedule within your facility includes electronic data in addition to paper. Guidelines for how long electronic data is stored are essential, so you do not keep data for longer than necessary and take up unnecessary space in your data repositories.

THE JOINT COMMISSION

The Joint Commission is the accrediting agency for health-care facilities including hospitals. The mission of the Joint Commission is to improve patient safety and quality of care. Many hospitals participate in the Joint Commission surveys in order to show the public that they take patient safety and quality seriously. The Joint Commission is an independent, not-for-profit agency.

The Joint Commission evaluates and accredits approximately 15 000 health-care organizations and programs in the United States. It has a comprehensive accreditation process that provides health-care facilities with standards and then evaluates the facilities on their compliance with the standards. The Joint Commission is recognized by the Centers for

Medicare and Medicaid Services (CMS) and any facility accredited by the Joint Commission meets the Medicare Conditions of Participation and can bill Medicare for services.

The Joint Commission has specific standards under the heading "Information Management" that relates to medical records. The principles of good information management apply to both paper-based records and EMRs.

INFORMATION MANAGEMENT (IM) STANDARDS

There are 13 IM standards which can change annually. The current list of 2007 IM standards are

Information Management and Planning

> IM.1.10 The hospital plans and designs information management processes to meet internal and external information needs.

Confidentiality and Security

> IM.2.10 Information privacy and confidentiality are maintained.
> IM.2.20 Information security, including data integrity, is maintained.
> IM.2.30 Continuity of information is maintained.

Information Management Processes

> IM.3.10 The hospital has processes in place to effectively manage information, including the capturing, reporting, processing, storing, retrieving, disseminating, and displaying of clinical/service and non-clinical data and information.

Information-Based Decision Making

> IM.4.10 The information management system provides information for use in decision making.

Knowledge-Based Information

> IM.5.10 Knowledge-based information resources are readily available, current, and authoritative.

Patient-Specific Information

> IM.6.10 The hospital has a complete and accurate medical record for patients assessed, cared for, treated, or served.
> IM.6.20 Records contain patient-specific information, as appropriate, to the care, treatment, and services provided.

IM.6.30 The medical record thoroughly documents operative or other high risk procedures and the use of moderate or deep sedation or anesthesia.

IM.6.40 For patients receiving continuing ambulatory care services, the medical record contains a summary list(s) of significant diagnoses, procedures, drug allergies, and medications.

IM.6.50 Designated qualified staff accept and transcribe verbal or telephone orders from authorized individuals.

IM.6.60 The hospital provides access to relevant information from a patient's record as needed for use in patient care, treatment, and services.

MEDICAL STAFF (MS) STANDARDS RELATED TO DOCUMENTATION

The standards that relate to medical records and documentation within the Medical Staff portion of the Joint Commission standards are

Standard MS.2.10 The organized medical staff oversees the quality of patient care, treatment, and services provided by practitioners privileged through the medical staff process.

Monitoring

The Joint Commission performs random unannounced surveys that typically occur every 2–3 years. It is wise for hospitals to form committees that address the standards of compliance on a regular basis, so there is continued readiness in the event of an unannounced survey. Furthermore, it is in the best interest for patient safety and quality when hospitals are continuously implementing processes in order to comply with the Joint Commission standards. The Joint Commission has made great strides in how they handle the survey process as in the past hospitals knew when to expect the surveys and would essentially cram for the test. The current method encourages hospitals to achieve ongoing compliance.

The Joint Commission has a method by which they rate hospitals and give timeframes depending on the severity of the noncompliance for the hospital to prove they are meeting standards. Hospitals are at risk for losing their accreditation if they are not able to achieve and maintain compliance with

Joint Commission standards. Losing accreditation could ultimately result in a hospital losing their ability to bill federal payers creating large financial implications for the institution. Maintaining Joint Commission accreditation is essential for the viability of the institution and the safety of its patients.

11

WORKING WITH ORGANIZATIONAL LEADERSHIP

JAMES FINE

Department of Laboratory Medicine, University of Washington, Seattle, WA

GRANT FLETCHER

Division of General Internal Medicine, Harborview Medical Center, University of Washington, Seattle, WA

BACKGROUND

The success or failure of health-care information systems (HCIS) in meeting the needs of an organization often depends more on leadership and organizational factors than a mastery of the technical issues. Health-care organizations (HCOs) have evolved into large, complex entities, with multiple information requirements. The capabilities of information technology (IT) likewise have expanded, and with this expansion have come new opportunities to improve patient care. Fitting the sophisticated technology to the diverse information needs of a dynamic organization can therefore be a daunting challenge. Moreover, the introduction of a HCIS can profoundly alter the process of how care is delivered. Technical considerations and organizational understanding therefore cannot be thought of in isolation (as has so often been the case), but must be integrated throughout the design and implementation of a HCIS.

Despite the clear need to address organizational and leadership issues in HCIS design and implementation, these areas often receive less attention than the technical aspects of IT. Compared to the scientific approaches and the hardware and software issues by clinical providers and IT professional, social and organizational considerations are less clear-cut [1]. There are insights from social science fields including sociology, anthropology, psychology that help us understand organizational structures and processes, but these disciplines provide few measurable and visible variables when applied to management. The literature on management of health-care organizations is driven more by coalescing experience from many cases in narrative form, rather than rigorous, data-driven empirical observations. Organizational change involves so many complex and dynamic factors that characterizing it defies application of universal and fixed principles [2]. What follows then are general themes of what appears to work based on narrative reviews, without presumption that these principles apply to all situations. Use of these themes in a particular context still requires the elusive qualities of insight, critical thinking, and judgment.

This chapter begins with an overview of how health-care organizations are structured in the United States—the evolution of HCOs to more complex and integrated systems, the IT decisions faced by the organizations, the components of a leadership team, and the stakeholders within the organization. We then turn our attention to what makes for effective leadership and management within the organization—qualities of effective leadership, barriers to implementation of a HCIS within the organization, and project management strategies for implementation.

THE EVOLUTION OF HEALTH-CARE ORGANIZATIONS

The history of how information systems have been used in healthcare is closely linked to the history of health-care financing and organization. After World War II, public and then private health insurance increasingly financed the delivery of care. Under a fee-for-service structure, from 1960 to 1980 the financial incentives of health-care delivery were to increase the volume of services, particularly highly paying specialized services. Information systems within hospitals were developed to track procedures and services provided to patients for billing purposes; data on costs and quality were not important factors for the financial health of the organization, and received minimal investment. From the 1980s onward there has been a gradual shift in the financial risk from third party payers (such and employer-based insurance, Medicare, and Medicaid) to patients, hospitals, and providers, as the costs of care continued to increase. In addition, there has been increasing recognition of shortfalls in the quality of healthcare. The Institute of Medicine's report in 2001 that estimated 100 000 annual patient deaths due to medical errors drew greater attention to this issue [3]. As a result there has been greater interest in using IT to improve the efficiency and quality of health care.

With the changes in total spending, financial incentives, and technology, health-care delivery systems have become more complex as well. The 1990s saw a flurry of consolidation of health-care institutions into integrated networks, comprised of previously separate functions. In many cases separate hospitals, clinics, rehabilitation centers, nursing homes, laboratory, and radiology centers became part of the same HCO as these organizations sought to improve their competitive position in the marketplace. With these change arose challenges to integrating previously separate information systems, as well as opportunities to improve the coordination of patient care.

Information systems have had increasing requirements and capabilities as well. Initially, information systems using mainframe computers were developed to automate tasks such as tracking procedures and other charges for billing, as well as payroll for the staff. In the 1970s, the use of information systems expanded to automate procedures within separate departments of hospitals such as laboratory, radiology, and pharmacy. By the 1980s, IT systems were developed to include some clinical processes such as order writing and some charting functions. These systems would generally be developed separately departments, so that within the same hospital there would often be separate software and hardware for overlapping information such as patient demographic data, and accessing the information would require separate terminals. In the 1990s, health-care delivery systems became increasingly integrated as HCOs encompassed a larger spectrum of institutions [4].

TYPES OF IT DECISIONS

The approach of a HCO to the integration of diverse health-care delivery systems is a strategic issue with far-reaching implications for the financing and management of care. Because the different hospitals, clinics, and departments within the HCO often developed relatively autonomously, they frequently suffer "silo syndrome," where they do not see the need to coordinate their own functions within the organization as a whole, and resist changes to that end.

The benefits of integration include improvements in the coordination of care and economies of scale for operational functions. When choosing hardware, operating systems, and applications across the organization, the advantages of centralization include control over security and quality of information, as well as avoiding redundancy of information as systems are integrated. Centralized systems do not confront as many problems with compatibility, making changes to the one system easier than upgrading the interaction among separate components. Data can be standardized, and the quality of the information can be controlled. On the downside, centralization of applications will usually not provide as much functionality and meet end-user needs, since specialized applications do not necessarily conform to the organizational standard.

There are gradations between these extremes, and some process can be integrated and others left decentralized. A matrix structure of organization, in which skill sets are centralized, but projects draw across departments and disciplines, is often desirable to strike a balance between centralized vs. local control. Crucial processes such as security, for example, should generally be unified to have control over access, with one security system and one unifying password. The quality of the access portals and timetable for password changes then can be controlled. Clinical data sharing and billing are also generally needed within the organization to coordinate care and administration. Outside of these domains, local control can often allow the necessary flexibility to meet specialized needs.

Another major strategic consideration in the design of information systems is how the organization can better control costs and increase quality. Thus new applications, or additional features to existing applications, may be needed. Examples include methods to integrate and display information for clinical decision support, such as identifying medication interactions; new data entry methods, such as computerized entry of medications and provider notes; and measures of outcomes and processes to modify care and improve quality. Applications must be carefully selected with user input and buy-in since the organizational process may change fundamentally with the introduction of such systems.

Beyond these broad strategic issues, there are numerous fundamental technical questions the organization must address (as are elaborated elsewhere in the book). Examples include should the electronic medical record be developed within the organization or purchased from vendors? How are priorities set for upgrades or replacement of hardware, operating systems, and applications relative to other organizational goals? What level of risk is appropriate in weighing access to data by providers vs. patient privacy? Should there be replacement of traditional hand-written orders and notes with computerized physician order entry and notes? These issues must ultimately be decided by the organizational leadership.

STAKEHOLDERS

There are numerous parties affected by the decisions within an organization, with different interests and power relationships. There are usually board members for the larger enterprise as well as for the individual hospitals. There are executive administrators (Chief Executive Officer, Chief Operations Officer, Chief Financial Officer, Chief Information Officer, and medical directors) both for the organization and the individual hospitals and large clinics. Physicians have played a prominent role in the decisions of HCOs, and historically department chairmen have had a great deal of autonomy and influence in academic medical centers. Multiple other departments and their respective leadership also must be considered (nursing, pharmacy, billing, laboratory, radiology). There are also other stakeholders exerting increasing influence on organizational decisions. Private and government payers have increasingly demanded organizational standards to ensure quality and control costs. Patients, the raison d'être of the organization, increasingly want a say in how care is delivered. As the scope of HCOs has enlarged, the challenges have increased for developing coherent organization policies.

INVOLVEMENT OF STAKEHOLDERS IN COMMITTEES?

The Leadership Team

Most HCOs designate a leader for information technology initiatives, such as the Chief Information Officer (CIO), who reports to the senior leader within the organization. The CIO often has been one with a technical background in information systems. In the past, information systems issues were delegated without careful integration into the overall organizational strategy, and the IT department would be run by its leader with relative autonomy. As the information systems in the HCOs have expanded, the skills and importance of the CIO perspective in executive decisions have extended well beyond the direct management of the IT department. Business, financial, and communication skills are now invaluable in CIOs, in addition to technical expertise. A CIO must fully grasp the strategic position and the larger environment in which the HCO operates to help guide decisions on IT investments. An IT leader in the HCO today should work closely with the other members of the administration in formulating overall strategy and budget decisions.

A major function of the CIO is to educate other members of the organizational leadership on key aspects health information systems that would influence strategic and operational decisions. The administration "hold the keys to the bank." The executive administration (such as the CEO, CFO, COO, and medical directors), as well as members of the Board of Trustees may not have significant background in IT and find it terrifying, given the risk and economic impact. Yet major decisions and responsibility for IT investment must be made by the highest levels of leadership in the organization, without deferring to the IT department, thereby taking ownership of the success or failure of the endeavor.

The role of the CIO is not only run the IT department well, but also to help clarify the priorities, tradeoffs, and budgetary constraints of any given course of action. The senior leadership need to know when there are critical hardware or software upgrades for the information system to operate smoothly, or when there are inescapable issues such as budgeting for electricity usage or appropriate cooling systems with expansion of the system servers. Learning to say "no" to the HCO leadership when necessary and educating on the realities of tradeoffs to information system capabilities within a budget are part of the job description for the CIO. And never forget the need to anticipate maintenance costs after a system becomes operational.

Some institutional design elements can facilitate communication. Having one of the board members with a background in IT may be helpful. External advisory committees comprising members of the administration leadership and IT department can open communication channels. Formalizing CIO communication, such as regular updates or scheduling special meetings or retreats, can keep all members of the administration abreast of developments [5].

Throughout the process of communication, the CIO should inform the leadership of specific IT issues, but also establish credibility and trust with the leadership. Specific issues to educate the administration on with any proposed IT initiative include ensuring the effort is well integrated into the overall organizational goals; ensuring risk factors such as patient confidentiality and system reliability are addressed in the plans; understanding the budget requirements of a project; and understanding how IT system changes will alter the processes of care. Since the organization's leaders may not have a technical background, the CIO should be aware of some surrogate markers of competence: communication with the administration in business terms; having a track record of success within the organization; demonstration of a good understanding of comparable efforts at other organization; and exhibiting an understanding of the health-care industry and forces influencing it [5].

Committees are also an essential means of communicating and planning within the organization. Committees have various purposes and audiences. A steering, or oversight, committee comprised of stakeholders in the organization should have at least one member with both IT experience and senior management experience. This member should ideally be able to communicate well the IT issues involved to other committee members in a language free of jargon, and have a holistic view of the organization. In addition, such a member should emphasize the opportunities and big picture rather than getting bogged down in details and barriers of the work [6]. Other committee may be subsets of larger governing bodies. There are some techniques to help committee communication. First, the method of interaction should determine the size—committees requiring interactive communication should be no larger than 6–8 people, while larger committees lend themselves to unidirectional communication only. Second, the purpose of the committee meeting should be clarified—is the meeting to discuss broad organizational strategy or a particular aspect of implementing a system? Third, barriers to implementation should be addressed, such as a resistant culture or lack of appropriate leadership [7].

ROLE OF CONSULTANTS

Consultants can play a valuable role in planning, selecting, implementing, and operating clinical computing systems. Their prior experience, can assist the health-care organization through what is often its first experience with a particular project. They can also add credibility to recommendations of internal committees because of this experience. Leaders should use consultants wisely because of their disadvantages: they often cost more than using internal employees; the knowledge they gain leaves with them when their engagement finishes; and they may lack the loyalty to the organization and knowledge of its history and culture.

QUALITIES OF EFFECTIVE LEADERSHIP

Management guidelines for organizational change are part of a larger discussion of how to formulate and implement an organizational strategy. The business literature is full of the latest fads and sweeping recommendations of what every manager needs to know. While HCOs are too complex and particularistic to extract definitive principles, there are some common elements that emerge and ring true [8–12].

Successful leadership of a HCIS requires a diverse set of skills in the conceptual, technical, managerial, and interpersonal domains [13]. To develop strategy that is consonant with the organizational goals, the leaders must see the larger context of the organization—the economic, political, and social forces shaping it. Within the leadership team, there must be technical competence, and a solid understanding of the hardware and software needs for the system. Administrative skills are needed to supervise the departmental IT staff as well as for the implementation of IT projects throughout the organization. Interpersonal skills are required to judge the capabilities of people to whom responsibility is delegated, build cohesive teams, communicate effectively, and share the mission and vision of the organization.

All these skills need not to be in one individual. Successful leadership in organizations often occurs with different members of the leadership team serving complementary roles [14]. For complimentary leadership to be effective, there needs to be a clear understanding of the respective strengths, roles, and responsibilities among members of the executive administration. For example, the CEO may act as a taskmaster for meeting schedules and budget, while the COO provides rewards and inspiration. Complimentary leadership does not imply a strict division of labor; all leaders need a similar core understanding of to be effective. Thus while the CIO may contribute technical knowledge to decisions, this knowledge must be well articulated and communicated among all members to develop a plan with a sense of shared ownership for the outcome.

BUDGETS

The process of budgeting, in which formal projections of anticipated costs are made, is a major component of the overall IT strategy for the organization. A portfolio of the various projects being implemented should be made. For each project, the financial profile, plan for updates, and sunset of the project is defined.

The elements of budgets are operations costs and new project costs. Operational costs refer to expenses for the information systems already in place—the staffing, facilities, contracts, and supplies. Maintenance expenses, such as software upgrades and hardware expansions or replacement, are also part of the operational costs. The budget for ongoing operations typically comprises the majority of the overall IT budget. Budgeting for new projects involves specifying both the capital investments (software, hardware, and staff for implementation) and the new operational costs the project adds to the overall expenses to determine the lifetime costs of the project.

The approval process for the budget can be quite cumbersome. At public academic medical centers such as ours, there are many layers of approval. This includes approval through the campus authority, the medical center, board approval, and final approval by the state government. Throughout the process there is ongoing auditing by an outside agency. Transparency and openness are advantages to this oversight; nimbleness and speed are potential disadvantages.

ADDRESSING SOCIAL ASPECTS
OF IMPLEMENTATION

A smooth and timely implementation of projects is an outgrowth of extensive and careful planning. During the planning phase multiple potential obstacles to implementation must be addressed. Among the issues to cover include: getting end-user involvement in the process from the beginning to ensure their concerns are met; identifying the workflow changes that may be introduced; formulating ways to accommodate these processes; involving champions for change to improve adoption; and understanding the cultural and political environment of the organization.

Working with end users at all stages of the process of HCIS development is one of the most important factors for successful implementations. Too often applications are designed separately from end-user input, and then the user is forced to fit the process. This is a recipe for failure.

Inattention to physician needs in designing and implementing electronic medical records, for example, can lead to outright rejection of the system. David W. Bates and colleagues have shared lessons from the implementation of decision support systems that are apropos of information system applications generally [15]. They highlight the importance of speed in decision support. Physicans strongly resist stopping what they are doing. Therefore the applications must respond quickly, the intervention must fit into the workflow, and information provided must be timely. Effective decision support is an iterative process, requiring ongoing feedback and monitoring of the impact of the system on the desired outcomes.

PROJECT MANAGEMENT

Leadership expects and is entitled to good project management. Formal project management techniques facilitate the implementation of a project. Project management is a systematic process for planning and implementing a project within a schedule and budget. The process begins with a definition of the project's scope, costs, and timeline [16]. The project then is broken down into smaller tasks, and responsibilities for each task specified. Software programs and diagrams help to further deconstruct the project into subtasks, visualize timelines, and calculate costs associated with the project [17]. Ideally, a project manager with a background in the process is available to lead the effort. Familiarity with both the organization and its people, as well as techniques of project management are beneficial. The process should be data driven. Feedback should be obtained throughout the implementation process: prior to implementation to establish baseline status and plan, throughout the implementation to measure progress, and on project completion.

Project management has defined planning, implementation, and post-implementation phases. Much of the planning phase, as described above, attempts to anticipate and address barriers to change, cultivating relationships and buy-in from users, as well as making sure systems meet user needs. With well-conceived and extensive planning, many of the pitfalls of implementation can be avoided. Essential to all the activity described above is the continuous education and communication to leadership as the project progresses. The importance of this to the success of this endeavor cannot be underestimated.

REFERENCES

[1] Braude RM. People and organizational issues in health informatics. J Am Med Inform Assoc. 1997: 4(2): 150–1.
[2] Glaser JP. Information technology strategy: three misconceptions. J Healthc Inf Manag. 2006; 20(4): 69–73.

[3] Medicine IO. Crossing the Quality Chasm. Washington, DC: National Academy Press, 2001.

[4] Vogel L and Perreault L. Management of information and healthcare organizations, in Biomedical Informatics: Computer Applications in Health Care and Biomedicine. Shortliffe, EH (ed.) New York: Springer, 2006, p. 1037.

[5] Glaser JP. The role of the board in the IT discussion. Trustee. 2006; 59(6): 17–21.

[6] Nolan R and McFarlan FW. Information technology and the board of directors. Harv Bus Rev. 2005; 83(10): 96–106, 157.

[7] Frisch B and Chandler L. Off-sites that work. Harv Bus Rev. 2006; 84(6): 117–126.

[8] Austin CJ, Hornberger KD and Shmerling JE. Managing information resources: a study of ten healthcare organizations. J Healthc Manag. 2000; 45(4): 229–38; discussion 238–9.

[9] Ash J. Organizational factors that influence information technology diffusion in academic health sciences centers. J Am Med Inform Assoc. 1997; 4(2): 102–9.

[10] Bernstein ML, McCreless T, and Cote MJ. Five constants of information technology adoption in healthcare. Hosp Top. 2007; 85(1): 17–25.

[11] Lorenzi NM, Riley RT, Blyth AJ, et al. Antecedents of the people and organizational aspects of medical informatics: review of the literature. J Am Med Inform Assoc. 1997; 4(2): 79–93.

[12] Lorenzi NM, Riley RT, Blyth AJ, et al. People and organizational aspects of medical informatics. Medinfo. 1998; 9(Part 2): 1197–200.

[13] Lorenzi NM and Riley RT. Managing Technological Change: Organizational Aspects of Health Informatics. Health Informatics Series. Hannah, KJ and Ball MJ. New York: Springer, 2004.

[14] Miles, SA and Watkins MD. The leadership team: complementary strengths or conflicting agendas? Harv Bus Rev. 2007; April: 90–8.

[15] Bates DW. et al. Ten commandments for effective clinical decision support: making the practice of evidence-based medicine a reality. J Am Med Inform Assoc. 2003; 10(6): 523–30.

[16] Project Management Institute. A Guide to the Project Management Body of Knowledge. 3rd edn. Newtown Square, PA: Project Management Institute, 2004.

[17] Hagland M. Methods to the madness. When it comes to quality improvement methodologies, CIO leadership will be essential. Healthc Inform. 2007; 24(1): 30–3.

CAREERS IN HEALTH CARE COMPUTING

12

CAREERS IN BIOMEDICAL INFORMATICS AND CLINICAL COMPUTING

DAVID MASUDA

*Department of Medical Education and Biomedical Informatics, School of Medicine,
University of Washington, Seattle, WA*

> *President Bush has outlined a plan to ensure that most
> Americans have electronic health records within the next
> 10 years. The President believes that better health information
> technology is essential to his vision of a health care system
> that puts the needs and the values of the patient first and gives
> patients information they need to make clinical and economic
> decisions.*
>
> The President's Health Information Technology Plan[1]
>
> *With the possible exception of internal medicine, has ever
> a health related discipline been lumbered with so inexpressive,
> so unexciting a label? We know what surgeons do, or proctol-
> ogists, or biochemists, but 'informaticists'? Blank looks and a
> few smirks all around the reunion mixer.*
>
> Milton Corn, Associate Director,
> National Library of Medicine

INTRODUCTION

Few would argue that the U.S. health-care system is moving slowly
but surely away from a record keeping systems based on paper and
toward electronic medical records. President Bush, in four consecu-
tive State of the Union addresses, has called for EMRs for most
Americans by 2014. Annually, tens of billions of dollars are being
invested in such systems by care delivery organizations ranging from
large multi-state integrated delivery systems to small one and

two-person physician practices. In short, clinical computing will be a major force of change in the health-care system in the coming decades. And yet the road to this goal, as we have learned, is littered with potholes. Arguably one of these potholes is that biomedical informatics, the discipline[1] that undergirds both research in and the practical application of clinical computing, is, as Corn observes, neither well-known nor well-understood. Therefore, a chapter describing careers in the field is in many ways an adventure into the unknown. There are a number of related reasons for this:

- Biomedical informatics is a discipline that suffers *from lack of a clear or widely accepted definition*. Most would agree that it is an "integrative field", combining aspects of clinical medicine and nursing, computer science, library and information science, organizational management, and other related domains. Yet how skills and knowledge in each of these contributes to any given job or job role is highly variable. Moreover, potential employers may—or may not—have a meaningful understanding of the value biomedical informatics specialists[2] can bring to the organization.

- Similarly, there are *several synonyms used to describe the scope of the field*—for example, "healthcare information technology" (HIT), "information systems/information technology" (IT/IS) and "information and communication technology" (ICT) to name a few. These terms tend to be used interchangeably across the industry although there may be significant differences in what is being described.

- While the number of biomedical informatics training programs in the United States is growing, with an increasingly rich range of educational objectives and experiences, there is to date *no widely recognized set of biomedical informatics credentials* that have common meaning to employers. The academic degrees available range from associate to doctoral, and the focus of study ranges from highly theoretical and research-based to highly applied and practical. There are a few certification programs for biomedical informatics specialists, but these are relatively new and not yet

---

[1] For simplicity's sake we've elected to use the term "biomedical informatics" throughout this chapter, with the intent to capture a range of related concepts, such as nursing informatics, medical informatics, patient informatics, health and related fields.

[2] Similarly, we'll use the term "biomedical informatics specialist" as a simplification of a large range of potential job skills and roles.

widely used as a measure of achievement. As well, formal accreditation of biomedical informatics training programs is in its infancy. There is currently no licensure specific to biomedical informatics specialists.

- The *current cadre of biomedical informaticist specialists* employed in this field come from a broad set of backgrounds including computer science, information science, information technology, clinical care, and others. Each of these brings a differing set of skills, knowledge, and experience. Hence, there is no single "flavor" that describes a biomedical informatics specialist working in clinical computing.
- Finally, our *knowledge of current and future clinical computing workforce needs is limited.* Research into workforce needs is now beginning to emerge, but as this is a rapidly evolving field, recommendations toward careers is based in good part on assumptions.

In short, advice as to how land a job in this field is not so simple as "get this degree and then send out your résumé." Rather, an exploration of career options will require some innovative thinking and a willingness to define for yourself the sort of role you might like to play, the activities you feel you would enjoy undertaking and the goals you envision achieving. There is no single clear path into clinical computing, and for the foreseeable future biomedical informatics specialists will come in many flavors. Nevertheless, there are a several concepts we can explore in some detail that may help you in this quest.

THE BIOMEDICAL INFORMATICS WORKFORCE

A discussion of careers in biomedical informatics and clinical computing ideally begins with an exploration of what we know about the current workforce as well as predicted future workforce needs. As described throughout this book, the discipline of biomedical informatics is a relatively young one—for most health-care organizations, clinical computing is a new venture. And as we've come to learn, in a discouraging number of cases the venture has been a painful one, in good part due to limited understanding of the necessary knowledge and skills to successfully develop and implement clinical computing applications, and as well the scarcity of people with the requisite capabilities to carry out such work. Both of these factors contribute to our relatively limited understanding of the biomedical informatics workforce. Simply put, if we have not agreed on a definition of the field, we'll have a hard time defining who we need to carry out the work therein.

Generally speaking, there is a belief that we will face significant workforce shortages in the near future. Speaking to the broad implementation of clinical computing systems across the country, David Brailer, former Director of the Office of the National Coordinator for Healthcare IT, noted, "We have a huge manpower crisis coming down the road [2]." In response, the American Medical Informatics Association (AMIA) has proposed that each of the 6000 hospitals in the United States needs clinicians—doctors and nurses—trained in biomedical informatics to lead the implementation and successful use of clinical computing systems [3].

In addition to clinician roles in clinical computing, there are growing needs for professionals skilled in "Health Information Management" (HIM), traditionally the domain of medical records departments in hospitals and clinics. The Bureau of Labor Statistics estimates that there were 136 000 employed HIM professionals in the United States in 2000, as well as a predicted growth in demand for HIM professional of almost 50% by 2010 [4]. The American Health Information Management Association (AHIMA), the national society of HIM professionals, believes this projected need requires significant effort at development of new and more advanced training programs for HIM professionals [5]. A 2001 survey [6] sponsored by AHIMA found that "There are insufficient numbers of certified professionals to fill all the positions and roles that need HIM competencies. Nearly 75% of the survey respondents indicated there are not enough qualified applicants to fill open HIM positions in their organization. Education was identified as being key to adapting to this changing role..." The authors concluded, "...while the need for a health information specialist work force is growing, the number of trained professionals is not keeping pace. Furthermore, no systematic plan exists for training the members of the current healthcare work force to use IT tools to do their jobs. Without a plan to train clinicians and existing health information specialists at all levels of healthcare delivery, the goal of an improved, interconnected healthcare system may never be met, and the industry may lose much ground in terms of quality, safety and efficiency as it moves toward an electronic future." In response to these findings, AHIMA, in partnership with the American Medical Informatics Association (AMIA), developed a set of nine recommendations [7] directed to industry, government and educators:

1. Adopt the vision of the Institute of Medicine "Crossing the Quality Chasm" report with its important role for health-care information technology to improve quality, safety, and cost-effectiveness of care. Use this vision to educate the health-care industry, employees, and employers at all levels that information technology is an integral part of health-care work.

2. Create incentives to align performance and reward systems in health-care practice environments to include informatics in professional goals and competencies, and encourage the health-care workforce to see health information competencies and skills as professional and personal goals.

3. Escalate industry-wide advocacy on a collaborative basis on the scope and importance of the health information specialist workforce and its significant impact on implementation of the electronic health record and information technologies throughout the continuum of care.

4. Build awareness of the important need for public and private sector funding and facilitating training of the health-care workforce to use health information technology through messages circulated among employers, associations, vendors, payers and the government.

5. Engage consumers as key stakeholders in the new health-care workforce by informing the public about the importance of health-care information technology and how it can improve the quality of health-care delivery to them.

6. Utilize innovative learning environments with robust health information systems for continuous delivery of education and training to the health-care information specialist workforce at all levels, and ensure access to training through multiple delivery methods including electronic learning formats.

7. Prepare a stronger health information specialist workforce for the future through formal education. Ensure facility competencies in the electronic health information environment. Market health informatics/information management/ information technology-related careers to young people to increase the number of qualified participants entering the field.

8. Disseminate tools for the health-care workforce through the sharing of information and best practices from other industries and from each other. Share best practices and understand culture changes from international colleagues that have implemented health information technologies.
9. Prepare the industry for patients who will increasingly manage their own health information and work with consumers and health professionals to educate them about the benefits, risks, and costs of personal health records.

While it remains unclear how much progress will be made on any of these recommendations, there are several key points for anyone considering a career in the field. First, an understanding of the core drivers toward clinical computing is important. Those captured by the IOM report—"...improve quality, safety, and cost-effectiveness of care..."—are key. Second, the notion of advocacy "...on the scope and importance of the health information specialist work force" suggests that job seekers are able to communicate to potential employers how and why trained skilled workers in these job roles is important. Finally, an understanding of the multiplicity and diversity of stakeholders in this transformation is critical. Significant progress in adoption of clinical computing will require active participation of a large range of players, meaning that the potential biomedical informatics specialist might do well to look beyond the traditional employers (hospitals and clinics) for opportunities.

Hersh [8] summarized another perspective on the workforce question, looking at the educational challenges ahead. Hersh noted, "A great deal has been written about the impediments to use of IT in health care. Issues such as cost, interference with clinical workflow, and technical support are often mentioned. But one area receiving little attention revolves around who will be the leaders in hospitals, physicians' offices, and communities where these systems are deployed. Furthermore, since the participation of physicians, nurses and other health care professionals is crucial for the successful implementation of these applications, how will such individuals be trained to provide them with the knowledge to work with IT professionals?" Hersh also argues that in additional to educational challenges, the issue of professionalism in biomedical informatics is important. To date, coordinated formal efforts to establish biomedical informatics as a recognized profession have been inconsistent. Hersh proposes the following five requirements as key to defining biomedical informatics as a profession:

1. An initial professional education in a curriculum validated through accreditation;
2. Registration of fitness to practice via voluntary certification or mandatory licensing;
3. Specialized skill development and continuing professional education;
4. Communal support via a professional society; and
5. A commitment to norms of conduct often prescribed in a code of ethics.

As with the recommendations from the AHIMA Workforce report, it remains to be seen how quickly progress will be made. In any case, for the clinical computing career aspirant we would recommend remaining on top of developments in this area. Membership and participation in professional societies is an important step in this direction.

There is limited data from training programs in biomedical informatics on the career experience of their graduates. Leven [9] reviewed the career paths of 1024 graduates from the medical informatics program of the University of Heidelberg/University of Applied Sciences Heilbronn, finding that 43% of the initial graduates were currently working within biomedical informatics, while 51% were working outside of the field (although in an informatics-related area). Of those who were working in biomedical informatics, about two-thirds reported their primary work roles to be in health-care information systems, with the remainder working in various specialty areas including "medical documentation, quality management, medical image processing, internet applications, telemedicine, bio-signal processing, knowledge-based methods/systems, and bioinformatics."

In an effort to discern the perspective of employers, Sable [10] surveyed information managers in 18 health-care organizations, inquiring about desired medical informatics training, prior work experience, skills for informaticists, and programming proficiency. He found "...a strong preference for informaticists with prior clinical work experience and an understanding of healthcare. Project management and data warehousing were highly rated skills. Informaticists were expected to know about health-care processes, clinical guidelines, and outcome management. They were not expected to be expert programmers." Sable concluded that "Healthcare organizations have complex information management needs that cannot be met by individuals who are trained in only one discipline. Medical informatics educational programs that have an applied healthcare focus are well equipped to train people for these roles. More studies need to be done in order to more fully understand the applied informatics needs of healthcare organizations. There is a role in healthcare organizations for interdisciplinary workers who understand clinical medicine, healthcare management, information technology, and who can communicate and work effectively across these organizational boundaries." Similarly, Hoffmann [11] surveyed potential employers of biomedical informatics programs graduates, asking about the most highly desired knowledge and skills. Most commonly cited skills included knowledge of the information used in clinical care, interpersonal skills, change management, relational databases, and project management.

In summary, several points should be clear. First, workforce needs now and in the future are not entirely clear, but it is a safe bet that there is a perceived need for a broad range of trained and capable biomedical informatics specialists as clinical computing projects move forward. Second, the specific knowledge and skills these specialists require span a broad spectrum—they require much more than simply "being a programmer." Third, it is increasingly likely that formal training in one or more "versions" of biomedical informatics will be a requirement in the future.

EDUCATION IN BIOMEDICAL INFORMATICS

While it is possible to move in to work roles in clinical computing without formal education—in fact a large number of biomedical informatics specialists working today have no such training—it seems likely that some level of advanced training will be increasingly desirable, and in many cases a requirement. In this section we discuss educational options, and the related issues of competencies and certification.

COMPETENCIES IN BIOMEDICAL INFORMATICS

In the last decade there have been several efforts at defining the knowledge, skills, and values—"competencies"—required by workers to be successful in various roles in clinical computing and biomedical informatics. Many of these projects have focused on specific individual work roles in healthcare, such as medical students [12], nurses [13, 14], public health practitioners [15], and more generally, information professionals [16] and biomedical informatics specialists [17]. A selected few are briefly summarized below.

Generally speaking, there are several points that bear mention in relation to how to interpret the research in competencies. First, there is often a significant degree of overlap in the competencies. This is understandable in that many, if not all, people working in clinical computing projects face similar challenges in these projects. Second, the methodologies used to develop the sets vary from project to project, and this likely has a direct effect on the nature of and relative importance rankings (when they exist). For example, it may not be a surprise that competencies as defined by educators in a biomedical informatics training program may vary from the competencies as defined by the future employers of those trainees. Third, with the relatively rapid evolution of this field, any defined set of competencies is likely to similarly evolve rapidly, especially those defined by employers. Given these caveats, perhaps the best uses of such lists are to give you a "personal checklist" with which to assess your current skills, strengths, weaknesses, and interests, and to enable you to evaluate the merits and fit of various training programs you may be considering. Therefore, we recommend that you obtain one or more of the competency lists from the resources listed below.

In "Pointing the Way," one of the largest studies of biomedical informatics competencies, Covvey[17] described biomedical informatics specialists as "...professionals that develop and/or deploy systems and methods based on information and communications technologies in support of health care, research, health system administration, and teaching." This definition is in differentiation to two other groups defined in the study—clinicians with health informatics (CHI) literacy who are the users of the systems in patient care, research, and teaching; and the research and development health informatics (RDHI) professionals who as researchers and teachers create new capabilities and produce new professionals. Most appropriate for our discussion is the third group—the "applied health informatics (AHI) professionals"—who implement, operate, and evaluate clinical computing systems in production environments. The competencies list was developed through engagement of clinical computing stakeholders including curriculum developers, teachers, potential and current students, employers in health and health-related industries, professional organization representatives, and potential certifiers of biomedical informatics professionals. The group produced "detailed lists of the macro-roles, of the micro-roles (functions) associated with each macro-role, of the detailed skills and knowledge (competencies) required to address each micro-role, of the experience components associated with each challenge, and of the mapping of challenges to macro-roles." For example:

- *Macro-Roles: Major organizational roles undertaken by IT professionals; functional positions. Examples: CIO, Manager of Systems, and Analyst.*

  - Challenges: Aspects of the health and/or systems environment requiring attention or intervention; incursions or difficulties to which the professional must respond. Examples: the need for planning, procuring, and evaluating systems.

- *Micro-Roles: Sub-functions/tasks that must be performed to address the challenges.*

  - Skills: Thinking, procedural, methodological, personal, or technical abilities required to successfully perform the specific micro-role. Includes the techniques, methods, templates, frameworks, etc. Mostly learned by doing.
  - Knowledge: Inter-related (elaborated) data, facts, meanings, concepts, and principles that provide the basis for understanding, comparisons, conclusions, decisions, advice, and the like. Mostly learned by listening, reading, and discussion.
  - Experience: Involvement in the application of knowledge and skills though discussions, projects, or work.

- *Competencies: The aggregate of skills, knowledge, and experience required to address a challenge.*

The complete project report contains highly detailed competency sets, as well as proposed education curricula that work toward developing the competencies in students.

Staggers[13] used a similar approach to set forth a set of competencies for nursing informatics, first gleaning from a literature review a master set of competencies that were then validated by a national panel of nurses with expertise in informatics. Her efforts resulted in a distilled set of competencies for four levels of nursing practice: beginning nurse, advanced nurse, nurse informatics specialist, and nurse informatics innovator. The following is a high-level summary of the findings—one should note that these likely apply in good part to non-nurse biomedical informatics specialists as well.

1. Beginning Nurse

    (a) Has fundamental information management and computer skills.
    (b) Uses existing information systems and available information to manage practice.

2. Experienced Nurse

    (a) Has proficiency in a domain of interest (e.g., public health, education...).
    (b) Highly skilled in using information management and computer technology skills to support their major area of practice.
    (c) Sees relationships among data elements and makes judgments based on trends and patterns within these data.
    (d) Uses current information systems but collaborates with the Informatics Nurse Specialist to suggest improvement to systems.

3. Informatics Nurse Specialist

    (a) An RN with advanced preparation possessing additional knowledge and skills specific to information management and computer technology.
    (b) Focuses on information needs of the practice of nursing, which includes education, administration, research, and clinical practice.
    (c) Practice is built on the integration and application of information science, computer science, and nursing science.
    (d) Uses the tools of critical thinking, process skills, data management skills (including identifying, acquiring, preserving, retrieving, aggregating, analyzing, and transmitting data), systems development life cycle, and computer skills.

4. Informatics Innovator

    (a) Educationally prepared to conduct informatics research and generate informatics theory.
    (b) Has a vision of what is possible and a keen sense of timing to make things happen.
    (c) Leads the advancement of informatics practice and research.

    (d) Possesses a sophisticated level of understanding and skills in information management and computer technology.

    (e) Understands the interdependence of systems, disciplines, and outcomes, and can finesse situations to maximize outcomes.

In an industry-centric model, the Health Leadership Alliance has developed a "HLA Competency Directory" [18]. The Health Leadership Alliance is comprised of several health-care professional societies with interest in clinical computing projects:

1. American College of Healthcare Executives;
2. American College of Physician Executives;
3. American Organization of Nurse Executives;
4. Healthcare Financial Management Association;
5. Healthcare Information and Management Systems Society;
6. Medical Group Management Association; and
7. American College of Medical Practice Executives.

The HLA effort was based on "...job analysis and input from the nation"s top professional societies representing more than 100 000 health-care management professionals. The project was undertaken by the HLA member organizations to ensure that health-care leaders are prepared for the future challenges they will face, and to determine the commonalities and distinctions in credentialing and professional certification among the various associations." Three hundred competencies were categorized under five major domains:

1. Leadership;
2. Communications and relationship management;
3. Professionalism;
4. Business knowledge and skills; and
5. Knowledge of the health-care environment.

The HLA web site offers a downloadable and searchable MS Excel® file of the full set of competencies.

    Finally, the National Health Service (NHS) in the United Kingdom has developed a set of competencies for a broad range of health-care workers [19]. The United Kingdom has undertaken a major effort in the past several years to provide electronic medical records for the entire country, and as such it is believed that a core requirement is "…enabling staff within the NHS to gain the skills and confidence to utilise both the technology and the information presented through this medium most effectively. It is therefore paramount that NHS organisations support their staff to develop Health Informatics skills and knowledge to improve the planning and delivery of healthcare. In response to the need to support the overarching modernisation agenda, the NHS Information Authority (IA) commissioned a piece of work which identifies the skills and knowledge levels required in Health Informatics for NHS professional staff…." The competency profiles in the NHS report delineate scales of competencies (from 0–4) for 18 different staff roles. These are categorized into 12 health informatics topics:

1. Basic Computing;
2. Basic Applications;
3. Computer Systems;
4. Data Quality;
5. Information Management;
6. System Development;
7. Strategic Development;
8. Clinical Informatics;
9. Communications Technology;
10. Security & Confidentiality;
11. Knowledge Management; and
12. Health Informatics Skills.

In summary, these varied competencies projects can be highly informative as to the breadth and depth of knowledge and skills in demand in the industry today, and in the future.

PROFESSIONAL CERTIFICATION

Ostensibly, competencies development is undertaken to direct curriculum development within educational training programs in biomedical informatics. At the other end of the education process is professional certification. Currently in the United States there are several certification programs in existence, each is sponsored by one or more professional organizations. These are summarized below.

The American Health Information Management Association (www. ahima.org) offers several levels of certification for people trained in HIM. These include certifications in:

1. Health Information Management

    (a) Registered Health Information Administrator (RHIA);
    (b) Registered Health Information Technician (RHIT).

2. Coding

    (a) Certified Coding Associate (CCA);
    (b) Certified Coding Specialist (CCS); and
    (c) Certified Coding Specialist-Physician-based (CCS-P).

3. Healthcare Privacy and Security

    (a) Certified in Healthcare Privacy (CHP);
    (b) Certified in Healthcare Privacy and Security (CHPS); and
    (c) Certified in Healthcare Security (CHS).

As to the benfits, AHIMA states that "Certification provides both personal validation and validation for employers and consumers of professional competence." Specifically, certification:

- demonstrates to colleagues and superiors a dedication to quality healthcare and to the highest standards for managing confidential health-care information;
- presents solid evidence to employers that an employee has trained and has been tested to implement best practices and apply current technology solutions, abilities that in turn advance the organization;
- sets a person apart from uncredentialed job candidates;
- assures current knowledge through continued education, possession of field-tested experience, and verification of base-level competency;
- holds value to employers because it supports a worker's ability to uphold industry standards and regulations, thereby potentially saving organizations from fines and penalties due to errors or noncompliance; and
- catalyzes career development by augmenting résumés and adding recognition to candidates' capabilities. Since credentials appear after a person's name, they announce expertise with every signature.

The eligibility requirements for AHIMA certification (using the RHIA certificate as an example) include

- Have successfully met the academic requirements of a HIM program at the baccalaureate degree level accredited by the Commission on Accreditation for Health Informatics and Information Management Education (CAHIIM) or the qualifications of such a program at the candidate's graduation must have met the requirements of the designated accrediting authority for an accredited program; OR
- Have earned a certificate of completion from a HIM program at the baccalaureate level, plus have a baccalaureate degree from a regionally accredited college or university. The HIM program must be accredited by CAHIIM, or the qualifications of such a program at the candidate's graduation must have met the requirements of the designated accrediting authority for an accredited program; OR
- Have graduated from a HIM program approved by a foreign association with which there is an agreement of reciprocity.

The *American Nursing Credentialing Center* (www.nursecredentialing. org) offers subspecialty certification in a number of disciplines, including health informatics. More than a quarter million nurses have been certified by ANCC since 1990. According to the ANCC, certification:

- validates your nursing knowledge and builds confidence. Nurse Managers believe that certification validates specialized knowledge, indicates a level of clinical competence, and enhances professional credibility;
- provides career opportunities and salary increases;
- are recognized and accepted by all state boards of nursing and by the U.S. military; and
- is the best measure of your ability to practice. ANCC certification shows that you have made continuing professional development a priority and an integral part of maintaining your ongoing competence to practice—providing evidence to the public and the profession of the strength of your nursing abilities.

The ANCC subspecialty certificate in health informatics is described thusly, "The informatics nurse is involved in activities that focus on the methods and technologies of information handling in nursing. Informatics nursing practice includes the development, support, and evaluation of applications, tools, processes, and structures that help nurses to manage data in direct care of patients/clients. The work of an informatics nurse can involve any and all aspects of information systems including theory formulation, design, development, marketing, selection, testing, implementation, training, maintenance, evaluation, and enhancement. Informatics nurses are engaged in clinical practice, education, consultation, research, administration, and pure informatics. The certification offering is also available to educators engaged in the education and supervision of graduate students in informatics nursing tracks and programs."

ANCC certificate eligibility criteria are

1. Hold a current, active, unrestricted RN license within a state or territory of the United States or the professional, legally recognized equivalent in another country;
2. Have practiced the equivalent of 2 years full time as a registered nurse;
3. Hold a baccalaureate or higher degree in nursing or a baccalaureate degree in a relevant field;
4. Have completed 30 hours of continuing education in informatics within the last 3 years;
5. Meet one of the following practice hour requirements:

   (a) Have a practiced minimum of 2000 hours in informatics nursing within the last 3 years;
   (b) Have practiced a minimum of 1000 hours in informatics nursing in the last 3 years and completed a minimum of 12 semester hours of academic credit in informatics courses which are a part of a graduate level informatics nursing program;
   (c) Have completed a graduate program in nursing informatics containing a minimum of 200 hours of faculty supervised practicum in informatics.

The *Healthcare Information and Management Systems Society* (www.himss.org) offers the credential of Certified Professional in Healthcare Information and Management Systems (CPHIMS). "A role delineation study was conducted to define the body of knowledge for the profession. The approach involved surveying members and nonmembers to identify tasks that professionals perform regularly and consider important to competent practice … The primary mode of delivery of the examination is via computer at over 110 Assessment Centers geographically located throughout the United States. The CPHIMS Certification is governed by the CPHIMS Certification Committee, a HIMSS committee of individuals with subject-matter expertise in the content tested on the examination. This Committee is responsible for assuring that certification meets high standards required for the profession; and is charged with setting general standards for the program, developing examination specifications, constructing new editions of the examination and establishing passing standards for the examination."

CPHIMS eligibility criteria are defined as follows:

> "To participate in the CPHIMS examination, a candidate must qualify under one of the following options."

- Baccalaureate degree plus 5 years of associated information and management systems experience*, 3 of those years in healthcare.
- Graduate degree plus 3 years of associated information and management systems experience*, 2 of those years in healthcare.

Associated information and management systems experience includes experience in the following functional areas: administration/management, clinical information systems, e-health, information systems, or management engineering.

As with competencies, the value of these certifications in the job marketplace is unclear—none appear to have become industry standards at this point.

EDUCATIONAL AND TRAINING PROGRAMS

The cornerstone of a career in clinical computing may well be set on the completion of advanced training in the domain. Fortunately, there are myriad programs from which to choose, and one has a broad range of educational options in terms of depth, focus, and instructional design. (AMIA curates a current and detailed listing of programs which is accessible at www.amia.org/informatics/acad& training/.) This variety of training programs does give you the freedom to consider several perspectives when considering options:

- *Depth.* Training options range from week-long, intensive "short courses" (offered by a number of entities such as HIMSS, AMIA, and the National Library of Medicine) to full PhD degree and Post-Doctoral programs. Between these are Master, Baccalaureate and Associate degrees, and graduate Certificate programs. Length of study therefore can range from a week to over 6 years.

- *Focus.* Programs have a broad range of focus, with varied goals and outcomes for graduates. One spectrum to consider is that of a research vs. an applied focus. Most PhD programs, for example, are designed to generate the next generation of academic researchers who will, through theoretical and applied scientific research, develop new knowledge in the domain. Conversely, most Masters and Baccalaureate degrees are "professional degrees", focused on generating graduates who will enter the clinical computing workforce, working in delivery organizations to deploy and operate clinical computing systems. However, we should stress that there is considerable overlap along this spectrum.

- *Instructional Design.* Many offerings are traditional in design, operating as in-residence, in-class degrees programs. However, in that a large number of prospective students are working professionals, executive format programs have also emerged, in which students attend courses in the evenings or on weekends. Also, distance learning programs are available, either as hybrid programs with both online and on-campus components or as a fully online component.

- *Domain.* Finally, programs generally have a core domain perspective. This may be in computer science, information science, health services management, nursing, medicine, public health, and others. Although programs may define themselves as biomedical informatics training program, in many cases each has a dominant domain strength and perspective.

In the following pages, we will highlight a small sample of representative programs.

Certificate Programs

Bellevue Community College in Bellevue, Washington has offered a 1-year Certificate in Medical Informatics since 2003 (bellevuecollege.edu/informatics/medical.htm) "Medical Informatics is the intersection of health care and technology. Although the field is relatively new, it has been ranked as one of the top five health-care careers by US News and World Report." The 3-quarter, 30-credit hour program is "designed for both working professionals and students who want to gain employment in this stimulating and emerging field. Individuals with backgrounds in healthcare or information technology fields are encouraged to apply." The program is fully distance learning-based, with optional twice monthly meetings on-campus. Learning outcomes for this program are defined thusly:

Upon successful completion of the program, you will be ready to:

- apply the essential concepts, theories, and models of health-care practice to real world applications;
- participate in successful project planning, analysis, design, implementation, and evaluation that involve both information technologists and clinical health-care providers;
- define, retrieve, and manipulate the data elements that make up effective health-care databases, such as Electronic Health Records and computerized patient order entry systems;
- evaluate medical computer software and enabling hardware, using established human factors principles;
- identify and apply high-quality health-care information found on the Internet and in health-care journals; and
- recognize current and future trends and issues that affect healthcare and Medical Informatics.

Sample courses include the following:

- Technology Fundamentals in Healthcare;
- Healthcare Informatics Standards;
- Healthcare Information Applications and Processes;
- Database Applications;
- Database Theory;
- Basic Project Management and Team Communication;
- Systems Analysis & Design;
- Project Management Applications;
- Computer & Software Fundamentals; and
- Medical Terminology.

Applied Masters Degree Programs

The School of Nursing at the University of Washington offers a Masters degree in Clinical Informatics and Patient-Centered Technologies (www.son.washington.edu/eo/cipct/). This program "...was developed with faculty partners from Biomedical and Health Informatics, Health Information Management, Health Administration, Computer Science, and Engineering and offers an interdisciplinary approach to systems, clinical informatics and patient-centered technologies." The program is a hybrid distance learning model, with both on-campus and online components, and generally takes 18 months to complete. This program is not limited to nurses—the students are interdisciplinary. Clinical internships are built into the program, giving students practical hands-on experience.

Learning outcomes include the following—"CIPCT prepares graduate students from multiple disciplines to implement and evaluate information technology (IT) and other cutting-edge tools to:"

- improve quality of patient care;
- manage chronic illnesses;
- increase patient safety;
- enhance communication between patients and providers; and
- increase efficiency of service delivery.

Sample courses include

- Introduction to Systems Thinking & Health Informatics;
- Managing Clinical Effectiveness;
- Database Concepts & Applications in Clinical Informatics;
- Scholarly Inquiry for Nursing Practice;
- Managing Health Systems;
- Foundations in Information Technology;
- Managing Organizational Effectiveness;
- Managing Access & Utilization;
- Practicum/Internship Informatics Project;
- Systems Design and Project Management;
- Healthcare Information Systems and the EHR;
- Informatics Capstone; and
- Patient-Centered Interactive Health Communication Technologies.

PhD and Post-Doctoral Programs

The School of Medicine at the University of Washington offers a range of degree programs in Biomedical and Health Informatics (www.bhi. washington.edu/). The program is described thusly: "At the University of Washington we define the field of Biomedical and Health Informatics (BHI) broadly, engaging students and faculty in a culture of interdisciplinary collaboration. Our research and training span a continuum of overlapping areas including biological, clinical, and population research. In addition to advancing the field of BHI itself, we are committed to contributing to the theory and practice of computing and information science, biomedical research, clinical care, consumer health, and public health. We also place an emphasis on translational informatics, the interaction of people and technology, and humanistic values in our work."

"For our teaching, we emphasize the following cross-cutting themes, which highlight our view of the field:"

- Understanding information problems and needs of people in biomedicine and health;
- Representing, using/applying, computing, and reasoning with incomplete, uncertain, and dynamic biomedical and health knowledge and data;
- Integrating, managing, sharing, and visualizing ever growing amounts of biomedical and health data and systems;
- Creating information systems that are useful for and usable by people, organizations and society, and that account for their behavior and values; and
- Evaluating and validating methods, models, tools, and systems.

Sample course work includes

- Introduction to Biomedical and Health Informatics;
- Public Health and Informatics;
- Biology and Informatics;
- Clinical Care and Informatics;
- Biomedical & Health Informatics Research Methods;
- Teaching and Communication in Biomedical Informatics;
- Knowledge Representation and BHI Applications;
- Biomedical Information Interactions and Design;
- Life and Death Computing;
- Computing Concepts for Medical Informatics;
- Bioinformatics and Gene Sequence Analysis;
- Critically Appraising and Applying Evidence in Health Care;
- Introduction to Systematic Reviews and Meta-analysis of Evidence; and
- Health Sciences Information Needs, Resources, and Environment.

EDUCATIONAL PROGRAM ACCREDITATION

In the same way that professional certification is a relatively new development in the field, accreditation of clinical computing and biomedical informatics training programs has been slow to emerge.

AHIMA sponsors the Commission on Accreditation for Health Informatics and Information Management Education (wsww.cahiim. org.) CAHIIM is "...the accrediting organization for degree-granting programs in health informatics and information management. CAHIIM serves the public interest by establishing quality standards for the educational preparation of future health information management (HIM) professionals. When a program is accredited by CAHIIM, it means that it has voluntarily undergone a rigorous review process and has been determined to meet or exceed the Standards set by the Board of Commissioners and curricula by the sponsoring professional organization – the American Health Information Management Association (AHIMA)." CAHIIM accredits HIM education programs at the masters, baccalaureate, and associate degree levels. The CAHIIM web site offers an interactive search tools to list accredited programs in the United States.

RESOURCES

This chapter should serve as a jumping off point for you to begin your exploration of career options in clinical computing and biomedical informatics. Delineated below are a number of additional resources that will prove valuable as you examine options for moving forward.

PROFESSIONAL HEALTH INFORMATION TECHNOLOGY/ INFORMATICS SOCIETIES

The American Medical Informatics Association (www.amia.org)

AMIA is known as the academic informatics group. It is "...an organization of leaders shaping the future of biomedical and health informatics in the United States and abroad. AMIA is dedicated to the development and application of biomedical and health informatics in support of patient care, teaching, research, and health care administration." AMIA has about 3500 members, including physicians, nurses, dentists, pharmacists, and other clinicians; health information technology professionals; computer and information scientists; biomedical engineers; consultants and industry representatives; medical librarians; academic researchers and educators; and advanced students pursuing a career in clinical informatics or health information technology. Members of AMIA have the option of joining one or more special interest "workgroups:"

- Clinical Information Systems;
- Clinical Research Informatics;
- Consumer Health Informatics;
- Dental Informatics;
- Education;
- Ethical, Legal, & Social Issues;
- Evaluation;
- Formal (Bio)Medical Knowledge Representation;
- Genomics;
- Knowledge Discovery and Data Mining;
- Knowledge in Motion;
- Medical Imaging Systems;
- Natural Language Processing;
- Nursing Informatics;
- Open Source;
- People & Organizational Issues;
- Pharmacoinformatics;
- Primary Care Informatics;
- Public Health Informatics; and
- Student.

Education Programs

AMIA offers a range of educational programs:

10×10.   First offered in 2003, the AMIA 10×10 seeks to train 10 000 professionals in applied health and medical informatics by the year 2010, to ... "strengthening the breadth and depth of the health informatics workforce." "Because we are serious about transforming our system of health care to be safe, efficient, timely, patient-centered, equitable, and effective, we must invest not only in technology, but also in the education and training of individuals to ensure our workforce is poised to meet this challenge. One of the factors most important to the success of health care information technology projects is the engagement and participation of clinicians. There must be a cadre of health care professionals (physicians, nurses, and others) who have knowledge and skills beyond their clinical training. Virtually every hospital, clinic, physician office, or other health care provider organization will in some way utilize information technology solutions in the coming years and will need health care professionals versed in informatics to assist with the implementation, use, and success of these systems." The AMIA 10×10 program is delivered in partnership with several universities across the United States. The courses are delivered through distance learning, providing the option of study for many. "The content will provide a framework but also cover plenty of detail, especially in areas such as electronic and personal health records, health information exchange, standards and terminology, and health care quality and error prevention."

"10×10 programs to be geared toward three major domains in the field of informatics:"

- Clinical or healthcare including personal health management; electronic and personal health records; health information exchange; standards and terminology; and health-care quality and error prevention;
- Public health/population informatics; and
- Translational bioinformatics.

Publications

The AMIA flagship publication is the bimonthly *Journal of the American Medical Infromatics Association* (JAMIA). JAMIA "…presents peer-reviewed articles on the spectrum of health care informatics in research, teaching, and application."

Career Services

AMIA offers an online Job Exchange, where members can browse "…job openings and find valuable employees and employers…The AMIA Job Exchange can help you find a position in the health care informatics field, or to fill a particular position in your organization." "The AMIA Job Exchange is a venue provided to members of the biomedical and health informatics community."

Meetings

AMIA holds two annual meetings, the Spring Congress in May and the Annual Symposium in November.

The Health Information and Management Systems Society (www.himss.org)

HIMSS is known as the trade organization in clinical computing—"the healthcare industry's membership organization exclusively focused on providing global leadership for the optimal use of healthcare information technology (IT) and management systems for the betterment of healthcare." HIMSS was founded in 1961, and currently has more than 20 000 individual members and over 300 corporate members. The goal of HIMSS is to "frame and lead healthcare public policy and industry practices through its advocacy, educational and professional development initiatives designed to promote information and management systems' contributions to ensuring quality patient care."

Educational Programs

HIMSS offers a range of professional educational program, including conference sessions at the annual meeting and online courses.

Publications

HIMSS publishes the *Journal of Health Information Management*, "…the only peer-reviewed journal specifically for healthcare information and management systems professionals." Published quarterly, each issue of the Journal examines a specific topic in the areas of clinical systems, information systems, management engineering, and telecommunications in health-care organizations.

Career Services

In terms of career development services, HIMSS offers an online web resource that includes the following:

- Interviewing Tips and Techniques;
- Online Job Search Tips and Tools;
- Resume Writing with sample Resumes and Letters;
- Specific Resources for the Military;
- Specific Resources for Students;
- Job Profiles; and
- Skills Assessment Exercise.

Meetings

HIMSS hosts an annual meeting each February.

The American Health Information Management Association (www.ahima.org)

AHIMA is the society representing medical records professionals, and as medical records move from paper-based to computer-based, HIM has become an important biomedical informatics organization. AHIMA is one of the oldest informatics professional societies in the United States, with over 80 years of experience. AHIMA has over 50 000 members, and is dedicated to "…advancing the HIM profession in an increasingly electronic and global environment through leadership in advocacy, education, certification, and lifelong learning." HIM professionals fulfill many roles in clinical computing, including work towards "…implementing electronic health records to adopting and implementing ICD-10 clinical coding systems to contributing to emerging issues like the creation of a national health information network."

Education Programs

AHIMA offers a distance education web site, with self-paced programs and courses such as:

- Clinical Terminologies & Vocabularies;
- Coding and Reimbursement;
- Compliance, Regulations, & Accreditation;
- Data Quality & Data Content Standards;
- e-HIM® & Electronic Records;
- HIM Operations;
- Privacy, Confidentiality & Security;

Career Services

AHIMA's "Career Assist Job Board" lists employment opportunities in HIM, including positions such as "Medical Records Management, Privacy Officer, Risk Management, Medical Coding, Corporate Compliance, and Data Analysis and Reporting." The AHIMA Informatics and HIT Workforce project documents define salaries and demographics.

Meetings

AHIMA holds an annual meeting each October. In addition there are several other regional and national meetings focusing on such topics as Education, Clinical Coding, Clinical Terminologies in Healthcare, and Leadership.

College of Health Information Management Executives (www.cio-chime.org)

CHIME represents senior executives in clinical computing and biomedical informatics. At more than 1100 members, "…CHIME is the premier association dedicated to serving the professional development needs of health-care CIOs and advocating the more effective use of information management in healthcare. Through a variety of education and networking events and research tools, our members stay connected with each other and stay on top of the cutting edge trends in the healthcare IT industry."

Educational Programs

CHIME offers a range of regional and national education programs, such as the "The Healthcare CIO Boot Camp", an "...intensive and highly interactive education program brings all of CHIME's knowledge and expertise to bear on developing the leadership skills healthcare CIOs need to be successful. The Healthcare CIO Boot Camp is built around a research-based model of CIO success pioneered by CHIME, called the CIO Success Factors. The CIO Success Factor model is founded on seven critical and developable skills that study showed are inherent in successful healthcare CIOs."

Career Services

CHIME members benefit from "...forums and other networking opportunities for members to meet and exchange information and experiences that support their professional growth and job performance." The CHIME web site also has a job posting service.

Meetings

CHIME holds its annual meeting each October.

Association of Medical Directors of Information Systems (www.amdis.org)

AMDIS is a relatively new organization in clinical computing, being founded in 1997. As the name suggests, it is "...the premier professional organization for physicians interested in and responsible for healthcare information technology. With our symposia, listserv, journal, on-line presentations, sponsored and co-sponsored programs and networking opportunities, AMDIS truly is the home for the 'connected' CMIO."

Publications

The Informatics Review (TIR) (www.informatics-review.com) is the e-journal of AMDIS. TIR is "...designed to allow busy medical and information system professionals interested in the latest academic developments in clinical informatics and computing to stay abreast of this rapidly evolving field. The Informatics Review seeks to promote the science of clinical informatics by publishing concise reviews of well-documented, peer-reviewed articles on a diverse range of clinical informatics topics from the leading medical and informatics journals."

Meetings

AMDIS holds its annual meeting in July.

JOURNALS

There are a large and growing number of publications that focus wholly or in part on clinical computing and biomedical informatics. This partial list should get you started.

- *Journal of the American Medical Informatics Association;*
- *International Journal of Medical Informatics;*
- *BMC Medical Informatics and Decision Making;*
- *Journal of Health Information Management;*
- *Healthcare Informatics;* and
- *Modern Healthcare.*

WEB SITES

There is an abundance of web resources covering every aspect of clinical computing and biomedical informatics. Two valuable web sites are "The Informatics Review" (*www.informatics-review.com/*) and "i-HealthBeat (www.ihealthbeat.org/).

CONCLUSIONS

As noted at the outset of this chapter, building your career path in clinical computing and biomedical informatics will in many ways be an adventure into the unknown. There are many routes one can choose to take, and the final destination may not be knowable in advance. There is an old cartoon depicting two young girls, standing in front of their school lockers, with one saying to the other, "I hope to grow up to be something that hasn't been invented yet." And so it may be for you.

In summary, we would suggest the following rules of thumb—seven "heuristics" to guide you in this journey:

1. *Get involved...*: Finding your way into the clinical computing workforce is more than a matter of getting a degree or credential. The oft-used adage of "It's who you know..." certainly applies. Reach out to a broad range of people and

organizations. Find and join local professional societies and clinical computing interest groups. If you currently work in a health-care environment, seek out those who currently work in clinical computing or biomedical informatics (and note that they may go by other titles) and find a route to working with them, as a volunteer if need be.

2. *Leverage your experience...*: Historically, the role a person plays in clinical computing is correlated with the role he or she played before going into this field. For example, a physician informatics specialist will likely be asked to fulfill a job role that integrates his or her clinical practice experience and relationships with the current and future needs of the informatics group. Such roles have often been considered the "boundary spanners"—and given the myriad professional and technical cultures in health-care organizations today, these roles are critical. Therefore, take your pre-existing experience or training in administration, project management, education, or consulting (to name a few), and leverage this skill and knowledge in the new role.

3. *Broaden your horizons...*: If your search to date has focused on a particular work environment, you may do well to explore more broadly. For example, if your work experience has been in care delivery organizations such as a hospital or clinic, you may do well to look at positions outside of delivery organizations. The range of employers is quite extensive and include, for example, clinical computing vendors, IT/IS consultants, pharmaceutical companies, governmental entities, health insurance companies, and other payers. Be forewarned that it can be a challenge to move from one employment environment to another. A nurse who has practiced in a hospital setting, for example, may find the work load, pace, and culture of the for-profit vendor world to be daunting—or exhilarating. Each of the potential work environments has distinct pros and cons, some of which are obvious and some of which not so obvious. Due diligence is in order.

4. *Sell yourself...*: Finding the right position will require more than a CV and a diploma. As noted earlier, the field of biomedical informatics is new and employers may have a wide range of what they consider informatics work roles to be. As well, there is limited (but growing) understanding amongst employers as to what an informatics degree enables one to do.

Therefore, you would be well advised to define and clarify for potential employers the specific knowledge and skills you can bring to their organization. Develop your "elevator speech." Consider building a portfolio of accomplishments in the field.

5. *Find a mentor...*: If you talk with successful biomedical informatics specialists, most will tell you they would not have achieved any success they currently enjoy without building upon the work of those who came before them and without learning from their predecessors. Many of the most significant lessons learned in this field come only as wisdom passed down from mentors to protégés.

6. *Consider the sort of work you really enjoy...*: You may find yourself fortunate and have a job offer delivered to you. Before jumping in with both feet, consider whether or not the work involved is what you really enjoy doing. This situation is one that can often face clinicians—in that there is a high demand for clinician informaticists; doctors and nurses may find they are invited to take on clinical computing roles based solely on their clinical credentials. And since the work involved is often dramatically different from clinical care delivery, such folks may realize weeks or months later that they are now enmeshed in a role in which they find little personal reward or fulfillment.

7. *Write...*: Finally, there will always be an audience hungry to learn from your experiences as you move down this path. One of the most effective means of furthering your own career is to share your stories and lessons learned with those following in your footsteps. There are many opportunities for writing—peer-reviewed journals covering clinical computing and biomedical informatics topics, trade journals, local and national newspapers and magazines, your company newsletter, or your own clinical computing blog.

In his book "*Why Things Bite Back: Technology and the Revenge of Unintended Consequences*," sociologist Edward Tenner notes "An account of technology's frustrations can start anywhere, but sooner or later it leads to medicine." As healthcare moves further down the road towards clinical computing, there is little doubt that frustrations will abound. Yet for most of us this is what makes the work so interesting and fulfilling. Despite the challenges ahead, we do hold firm to the belief that our efforts in this field will pay dividends, both in terms of a betterment of the health-care system and personal fulfillment in having contributed to the process.

Bon voyage...

REFERENCES

[1] http://www.whitehouse.gov/infocus/technology/economic_policy200404/chap3.html.

[2] Anonymous. Goal: teach I.T. to future clinicians. Health Data Manag. 2004; Available at http://healthdatamanagement.com/html/PortalStory.cfm?type=trend&DID=12037.

[3] Safran C and Detmer DE. Computerized physician order entry systems and medication errors. JAMA. 2005; 294: 179.

[4] Hecker D. Occupational employment projections to 2010. Monthly Labor Rev. 2001; 124: 57–84.

[5] Dixon-Lee C, Patena K, Olenik K and Brodnik M. Graduate education bridges the gap between the electronic health record and clinical need. J Healthcare Inform Manag. 2004; 18: 19–25.

[6] AHIMA. Data for Decisions: The HIM Work force and Workplace: Recommendations to the AHIMA Board of Directors. Chicago: AHIMA, 2004. Available at www.ahima.org.

[7] AHIMA Building the Workforce for Health Information Transformation. Chicago: AHIMA, 2006. Available at www.ahima.org.

[8] Hersh W. Who are the informaticians? What we know and should know. J Am Med Inform Assoc. 2006; 13(2):166–70.

[9] Leven FJ, Knaup P, Schmidt D and Wetter T. Medical informatics at Heidelberg/ Heilbronn: status-evaluation-new challenges in a specialised curriculum for medical informatics after thirty years of evolution. 2004; Int J Med Inform. 2004; 73(2):117–25.

[10] Sable JH, Hales JW and Bopp KD. Medical informatics in healthcare organizations: a survey of healthcare information managers. Proc AMIA Symp. 2000; 744–8.

[11] Hoffmann S and Ash J. A survey of academic and industry professionals regarding the preferred skillset of graduates of medical informatics programs, in MEDINFO 2001— Proceedings of the Tenth World Congress on Medical Informatics. London: IOS Press, 2001, pp. 1028–32. Peacock Publishers, 1971.

[12] Anonymous. Contemporary issues in medicine: medical informatics and population health. Washington, DC: American Association of Medical Colleges, 1998.

[13] Staggers N, Gassert CA and Curran C. A Delphi study to determine informatics competencies at four levels of practice. Nurs Res. 2002; 51: 383–90.

[14] Curran CR. Informatics competencies for nurse practitioners. AACN Clin Issues. 2003; 14: 320–30.

[15] O'Carroll PW. Informatics competencies for public health professionals. Seattle: Northwest Center for Public Health Practice, 2002.

[16] Anonymous. Health informatics competency profiles for the NHS. London: National Health Service Information Authority, 2001.

[17] Covvey HD, Zitner D, Bernstein RM. Pointing the way. Competencies and Curricula in Health Informatics. http://www.informatics-review.com/thoughts/pointing.html. Accessed Nov 19, 2007.

[18] www.healthcareleadershipalliance.org.

[19] www.nhsia.nhs.uk/nhid/pages/resource_informatics/hi_competencyprofiles.pdf.

INDEX